When World War II erupted, fifteen-year-old Louis Rubin pedaled his bike down to the Charleston harbor to see whether a German freighter might have come there to escape British warships, as had occurred in 1914. Although he went home disappointed, young Louis never lost his fascination with matters military.

Now one of America's most esteemed literary scholars, Rubin again turns his thoughts to history—particularly military history—by sharing his lifelong interest in the First World War and its aftermath. *The Summer the Archduke Died* offers essays, beginning with the outbreak of the Great War in Europe in 1914 and covering events of subsequent years, that examine historical issues in a fresh way. These essays take in a panoramic view of German militarism, the American role in the war, and British and American politics and politicos. They convey the impact of the war on writers and include a critical review of Theodore Roosevelt's life and legacy.

Rubin brings a keen eye for controversy to such matters as the battle of Jutland and Churchill's stance on the war with Hitler. In a provocative essay on the New British Revisionism, he not only debunks recent criticism of Churchill but also examines the decline of the British class system. In "Ladies of the British Establishment," he contrasts the politically notorious Mitford sisters with

THE SUMMER THE
Archduke Died

THE SUMMER THE
Archduke Died

Essays on Wars and Warriors

Louis D. Rubin, Jr.

University of Missouri Press Columbia and London

Library of Congress Cataloging-in-Publication Data

Rubin, Louis Decimus, 1923–
    The summer the Archduke died : essays on wars and warriors /
Louis D. Rubin, Jr.
        p. cm.
    Includes bibliographical references and index.
    Summary: "Writer and literary scholar Rubin turns his thoughts
to World War I and its aftermath, a subject of lifelong fascination for
him. Topics range from tactics used at the naval battle of Jutland, to
critiques of revisionist histories of Winston Churchill, to the war's
impact on literature"—Provided by publisher.
    ISBN 978-0-8262-1810-0 (alk. paper)
    1. World War, 1914–1918.   2. World War, 1914–1918—Influence.
I. Title.
    D521.R76 2008
    940.3—dc22

                                                        2008015843

Designer: Jennifer Cropp
Typesetter: The Composing Room of Michigan, Inc.
Printer and binder: The Maple-Vail Manufacturing Group
Typefaces: Palatino and Bembo

For John and Joanne Eisenhower

Contents

Preface

The essays in this book have to do mainly with the history of the First World War and the several decades afterward. They deal with the outbreak of war in Europe in 1914, German militarism, the naval Battle of Jutland, the American role in the war, British and American politics and politicos, the English Establishment then and afterward, the latter-day revisionist assault upon Winston Churchill, and the impact of the war on writers.

As such, they touch on matters that I have been reading and thinking about for much of my life. At the same time, they are not concerned with Southern or American literature, or the workings of the creative imagination, which are the topics to which a major portion of my professional writings have been devoted. I may add that the contents of this book were written following my retirement from teaching and publishing.

Upon gathering these pieces together it seemed to me that it would not be amiss to comment on the circumstances that impelled me to devote so much time and effort to reading and thinking about military history. Surely the community in which I grew up and my youthful place within it were not without their influence. An explanation seemed appropriate—not exactly an apologia, but in any event a How Come? So I have ventured to begin with some musings on the subject.

When I was ten years old, I was given an Underwood No. 5 typewriter, in part so that I would cease using my father's portable. Over the years since then, which have not been few, I have grown accustomed to doing my thinking at a keyboard. These days the keyboard is attached to a computer, but it remains my principal medium for discovering what I think about anything.

Most of the pieces in this collection were written as review essays, and bear the marks of their origins. As such they use one or more newly published books as their takeoff point for more general discourse. Because the essays were written independently of each other over a period of time, some repetition in phrase and thought was inevitable. I have tried to thin it out for this book, but doubtless much remains.

John and Joanne Eisenhower provided close readings and comments on several of the pieces in this book. Samuel R. Williamson, Jr., helped me with the title essay entitled "The Summer the Archduke Died," of which the title and the epigraph are taken from a sestina by my friend the late Howard Nemerov. John Shelton Reed helped me track down some information cited in the first chapter.

I am grateful to George Core, editor of the *Sewanee Review* and longtime friend; to the late Staige Blackford, for many years editor of the *Virginia Quarterly Review*; and to the present editor of that magazine, Theodore Genoways, for essays that in their original form appeared in those magazines. As first titled, they are:

"When the Archduke Died," *Sewanee Review* 110, no. 4 (Fall 2002): 688.

"'The Weasel's Twist, the Weasel's Tooth': The First World War as History," *Sewanee Review* 103, no. 3 (Summer 1995): 429–39.

"The Continuing Argument over Jutland," *Virginia Quarterly Review* 77, no. 4 (Autumn 2001): 583–602.

"The Great War: Three Works of Military History," *Sewanee Review* 108, no. 4 (Fall 2000): 624–39.

"Literature and the Great War," *Sewanee Review* 100, no. 1 (Winter 1992): 131–41.

"T. R.," *Virginia Quarterly Review* 81, no. 1 (Winter 2005): 257–62.

"Did Churchill 'Ruin the Great Work of Time'?: Thoughts on the New British Revisionism," *Virginia Quarterly Review* 70, no. 1 (Winter 1994): 59–78.

"Ladies of the British Establishment: The Mitford Sisters and Violet Bonham Carter," *Sewanee Review* 111, no. 2 (Spring 2004), 285–94.

Several of these essays were included in an earlier collection of mine, *Babe Ruth's Ghost* (University of Washington Press, 1996).

Finally, some of the material in the first essay in this book had its inception in two pieces written for *Southern Cultures:* "The Southern Martial Tradition: A Memory," 1, no. 2 (Winter 1995): 265–80, and "General Longstreet and Me: Refighting the Civil War," 8, no. 1 (Spring 2002): 21–26.

L.D.R.
Chapel Hill, North Carolina
March 2008

THE SUMMER THE
Archduke Died

1

A Certain Day in 1939

(2007)

Did all the lets and bars appear
    To every just or larger end,
Whence should come the trust and cheer?
    Youth must its ignorant impulse lend—
Age finds place in the rear.

—*Herman Melville, "The March into Virginia"*

When in September of 1939 the news came that Great Britain and France had declared war after Germany invaded Poland, I borrowed my father's binoculars and headed downtown to the Charleston waterfront.

Twenty-five years before, on the day in 1914 that war had broken out in Europe, a German freighter had entered the harbor seeking sanctuary from British warships. If anything like that were to happen again, I wanted to be there to watch.

The downtown waterfront was quiet when I arrived and mounted the sea wall at the Battery. The channel to the ocean out beyond

Fort Sumter was empty except for a fishing craft or two. The White Stack tugboats were tied up at Adgers Wharf. A small open-decked ferryboat droned its way across the harbor toward Sullivans Island.

No ships, belligerent or otherwise, showed up that morning. After waiting around for several hours I stepped back down to East Bay Street, climbed aboard my bicycle, and pedaled for home. War, and expectations of war, seemed a long way off.

Within less than three years' time, anyone who might arrive at the waterfront with a pair of binoculars or a camera would at once have been stopped and interrogated. The Battle of the Atlantic, the bombing of Pearl Harbor, America's entry into the war, and the Allied invasion of North Africa transformed the long-somnolent port of Charleston into a beehive of activity. Centered on and about the harbor were the Navy yard, commercial drydock and ship repair facilities, a Port of Embarkation, an ordnance depot, a naval weapons station, an Army hospital, an air base, and other military and naval installations. Ship watching was not only not encouraged; it was suspicious activity. But on that day in September, 1939, there was nothing in sight to suggest what lay ahead.

I was several months short of my sixteenth birthday and a rising senior in high school when war broke out in Europe. I am not sure just what it was that I was hoping to see out in the harbor that morning. Very likely I had a vision of a fleeing freighter steaming frantically through the jetties at the channel entrance, with British warships in hot pursuit. If so, my sympathies would have been all with the pursuers.

In those years, talk of wars past and present, displays of patriotic sentiment, and praise for the martial virtues in general were very much a part of the Charleston scene. My father, who was very high on civic activities, customarily took the family to witness public events. We seldom missed a ceremonial opening, the dedication of a monument, a parade, or a historical celebration. When an early eighteenth-century cannon was unearthed and excavated on Longitude Lane not far from the sea wall, we drove down to see it. When a monument to the Confederate defenders of the harbor in 1861–1865 was unveiled, we were there. When the keels of several gunboats were laid at the long-idle Charleston Navy Yard, we were on hand to watch. And so on.

The premier historical event in Charleston's history, which in significance and attention received outshone even the successful defense of the harbor against British naval attack in 1776, was the bombardment of Fort Sumter in 1861 that touched off the Civil War. From the balconies and rooftops of the homes just across East Bay Street, the local citizenry had watched artillery from various points around the harbor open fire on the fort, in clear view on a shoal at the harbor entrance.

As all youths in South Carolina knew, the Union garrison had surrendered after a brief, bloodless battle, and thereafter the fort, with a Confederate garrison manning its ramparts, withstood ironclad attacks and forays from adjacent beaches during four years of war and blockade. As a child in elementary school I had learned to recite Henry Timrod's "Magnolia Cemetery Ode":

> Stoop, angels, hither from the skies!
> There is no holier spot of ground
> Than where defeated valor lies
> By mourning beauty crowned!

In that poem, written in the year after the war ended, the prediction was made that the day would come when a monument to the Confederate defenders overlooked the harbor. Thanks to the results of that war, there were no funds available for such a purpose for long decades afterward. Not until the 1920s did a local citizen of large wealth, of which there were very few, provide the money for a commemorative statue, which was ordered from France and in the autumn of 1932 installed at the point of the Battery.

I was in attendance that day with my family for the unveiling. I was not quite nine years old. The bronze sculpture, mounted upon a tall marble pedestal, featured a naked warrior, muscles tensed, positioned with sword and shield to defend a robed female figure emblematic of the city of Charleston. Displayed on the warrior's shield was the state seal of South Carolina.

When the white cloth drape concealing the statue was removed, it became snagged on the warrior's outstretched sword, and someone had to be boosted up the pedestal to complete the unveiling. There was also some local perturbation because the heroic-sized warrior's anatomy was very much in view. Although the Great Economic Depression was then at its nadir and the city exchequer at lowest ebb, the elected authorities hastily authorized the addition of a bronze fig leaf.

Among those in the audience that day were a few white-bearded Confederate veterans and a considerably larger number of veterans of American participation in the First World War, my father among them. The events of 1917–1918 were still fresh in the minds of most of those looking on. I have no memory of what was said in homage to the valor of the city's Confederate defenders, but I have no doubt that the soldiers and sailors of both conflicts were included in the oratorical tributes. To quote from a booklet written several years later by a local veteran of 1917–1918, "America knew that from a high Valhalla, ethereal forms in blue, arm and arm with their grey clad countrymen, with differences long forgot, had joined in a triumphant p[a]ean of praise to the God of Battle, and then in proud unison, looked down to pronounce a benediction on this united land" (Major Alfred H. von Kolnitz, *The Battery in Charleston, South Carolina* [1937], 34).

My immediate family were relative latecomers to the local community as such matters were reckoned in Charleston, and my only personal connection with the Confederate heritage consisted of a great-uncle by marriage who had served in a South Carolina regiment, and who had died some years before I was born. Be that as it may, my father and several of my uncles and aunts were thoroughly caught up in the local pieties.

In retrospect this scarcely seems surprising. They were the progeny of mid-nineteenth-century immigrants with few or no surviving ties with the past across the ocean. As Reform Jews they were also cut off from so much of the social and cultural routines of the traditional Jewish community. Thus there was abundant incentive for them to identify with the secular loyalties of their community.

In the South, and certainly in an old seaport city such as Charleston, there was considerable encouragement to do so. This is not the place for a discourse on the sociology, or perhaps the cultural anthropology, that was involved. It will suffice to say that, provided certain distinctions were recognized and obligations accepted, civic and political participation was expected. In any event, community membership and its accompanying allegiances were pervasive and highly potent forces in those years, and in my own family's instance they appear to have come upon very receptive ground.*

So when the war of 1861–1865 and the Confederate military heritage were at issue, it was Us against Them, the Them being the Yankees. This was customary among almost all Southern children of my generation, whatever their immediate antecedents, during the years when I was growing up—almost all white children, that is. It would never have occurred to me or any of my contemporaries to question our inherited fealty to the memory of the Lost Cause. Ideology had next to nothing to do with it.

The earliest dream I can remember is of soldiers. It happened sometime in the late 1920s. A pathway in Hampton Park led through a gap in a wire fence next to trees and thickets, with narrow, dark green wooden posts on each side. As I watch, a soldier materializes from one gatepost, marches across the open pathway, and disappears into the other post. He is followed by another, and another, walking silently across the pathway in single file, never more than one in view at a time, to vanish into the gatepost.

There is a haziness to the image—dark trees and shrubs, the shadows, the gravel pathway, the soldiers, who though dressed in the U.S. Army uniforms I had seen at parades downtown on King Street were definitely Confederates. A veterans reunion may have been taking place in Charleston, and perhaps I had been told that I might see Confederate soldiers in the park that afternoon. That any such would be old men in their late eighties or nineties would not have been clear to me.

No small factor in the martial tradition that permeated the local atmosphere was the presence, to the west of Hampton Park not far from our home, of the campus of The Citadel, the Military College of South Carolina. On Friday afternoons there was a dress parade, to which as a small child I was always taken by a nurse. The corps of cadets, passing in review in their gray uniforms, with plumed shakos and chinstraps, polished belt buckles and buttons, the officers with swords and sashes, arrayed by platoons and companies

*I have written about this elsewhere at some length. See *The Golden Weather: A Novel* (1961), *Surfaces of a Diamond: A Novel* (1981), *Small Craft Advisory* (1991), and *My Father's People: A Family of Southern Jews* (2002).

with guidons and pennants, the band marching past with drums throbbing and horns glinting in the sunshine, made for an exciting afternoon.

Inevitably, when the last platoon swung by the reviewing stand and the time for the retreat ceremony neared I grew uneasy, for the salute gun was soon to be fired, and I did not care for explosions. Once the cannon blast came and the flag began its descent from the flagpole, however, the band broke into the Star-Spangled Banner and my martial ambitions were speedily renewed. To grow up to be a Citadel cadet one day was the ideal not only for myself but for every male child in our neighborhood.

In June of 1932 I was present for the last major Confederate reunion. We were staying in Richmond, the wartime capital of the Confederate States of America, where my mother had grown up, while my father convalesced from surgery. Each afternoon he went for a walk, and sometimes I was taken along. Several times we stopped by the Old Soldiers' Home, where there were cannon for me to climb on while my father chatted with the aged men in gray uniforms seated outside on benches.

While we were in residence, what was generally understood would be the last reunion of the United Confederate Veterans took place there, exactly seventy-five years after the Seven Days' Battles to the east of Richmond. Close to fifteen hundred surviving Confederates, the youngest an eighty-two-year-old wartime drummer boy, arrived aboard special trains from throughout the South. Battle flags flew everywhere, and the downtown streets and stores were festooned in gray, red, and white crepe bunting.

The culminating event was a parade along Monument Avenue, which I watched with my father from the sidewalk not far from the equestrian statue of Stonewall Jackson. There were U.S. Army, Navy, Marine, and National Guard units; a variety of bands and drum-and-bugle corps; police motorcycle squads; floats; and carloads of governmental and convention dignitaries. Last in the procession, installed in open touring cars, came the Confederate veterans themselves. They rode along in their gray uniforms, nodding and waving canes and broad-brimmed hats to the spectators lining the sidewalks. As the vanguard of the old soldiers drew near there was a hush. Then, just as my father called out "Give the old boys a

hand!" a mighty cry welled out from the crowd. The thunderous ap-
plause was sustained as car after car of Confederate veterans rolled
past while the present-day citizenry shouted their tribute.

I was eight years old then, but I took in what was going on. It was
an outpouring of pride in and love for the South's long-ago defenders. And these were *my* people—the old soldiers in the touring cars,
soon to depart the scene for good; the applauding crowds along the
parade route; the bands and the music. I may not have understood
the implications of the relationship or been able to articulate any of
its complexity, but I could feel the hair standing up on the back of
my neck—seventy-five years ago as I write this.

Back in South Carolina after my father's recovery we sometimes
went on Sunday afternoon family drives up to the Charleston Navy
Yard, were given a visitors card by Marine Corps guards stationed
at the gates, and drove around to see any warships that might be in
port. The Civil War made its memories felt there, too, for tied up along-
side one dock was the USS *Hartford*, Admiral Farragut's wooden-
hulled flagship at the Battle of Mobile Bay. Stripped of its masts and
rigging and empty of engines, it was at the yard for eventual repair
and refurbishing. We could go aboard, climb up to the bridge, and
even shout through the speaking tube to the engine room below,
"Damn the torpedoes! Full speed ahead!"—which I always made
sure to do despite the admiral's regrettable wartime affiliation.

It was not that the Confederate heritage was the only outlet for my
military enthusiasm. So far as martial events went, the First World
War held almost equal appeal. My father had been a sergeant in the
Marine Corps. I knew the words of the Marine Hymn by heart, including the verse about Chateau-Thierry and the Forest of Belleau.
One of my uncles, an Army lieutenant, was severely wounded in action during the Argonne Forest offensive. A large framed certificate
on the wall bore his name and rank and showed a helmeted Dough-
boy kneeling before a robed matron—very much like the one on the
Confederate statue downtown on the Battery—who was brandish-
ing a large ceremonial sword over him. Another uncle, my mother's
brother in Richmond, had suffered shrapnel wounds on his hands
and wrists, which he could make puff up by clenching his fists.

My father was an active member of American Legion Post No. 10,

to which in those years, in Charleston at least, no political implications were attached. In the early 1930s a unit of the Sons of the American Legion was formed, and I was duly enrolled, but so far as I know
it convened only once, after which no more was heard about it.

My father's Marine Corps uniform from 1917–1918 was stored in
our attic, and at the Army-Navy Store on King Street one could buy
surplus cartridge belts, bayonets, canteens, steel helmets, leggings,
gas mask containers, and other surplus wartime paraphernalia. An
Army sergeant at The Citadel, a friend of my father's, presented me
with a rifle stock and a saber and scabbard.

The newsstands downtown displayed an array of magazines with
garish covers, chronicling the aviation exploits of the Western Front,
nonfictional and fictional both, under such titles as *G-8 and His Battle Aces, Air Trails,* and, my favorite, *Flying Aces.* We built balsa models and disputed the merits of the various fighter planes. I knew the
names of the leading aces, and how many enemy planes each was
credited with having shot down.

For my twelfth birthday I requested and was given a book entitled
The Red Knight of Germany, by Floyd Gibbons, chronicling the career
of Manfred von Richthofen, who during the war had brought down
eighty Allied warplanes, mostly British, before being himself shot
down and killed. Each of his aerial triumphs was described, including his official reports, letters from those of his victims who survived, and the letters he dutifully wrote home to his mother, beginning "Liebe Mamma" and modestly describing his deeds and his
awards.

By the time I began reading and rereading the account of the Red
Baron's exploits, Hitler and the Nazis had come into power in Germany. I assured myself that a true nobleman and hero like Richthofen would never have condoned, much less supported, the Nazis.
The ability to reach conclusions in disregard of evidence to the contrary was a talent of mine in those years.

Not least of my aspirations as a teenager was in sports. I played
baseball, football, basketball, tennis, and golf, and in each my skills
ranged from mediocre to inept. What I was good at was reading and
writing about them. Yet I was convinced that through some abrupt,
mysterious process of transformation I would undergo overnight
metamorphosis into athletic stardom.

In the same way, as the war news from Europe grew ever more ominous even as I entered my late teens, it did not concern me that the same talents, or lack of them, that served to frustrate my athletic aspirations might likewise limit my military capabilities. When at age sixteen I became a college freshman, I did concede that it was probably just as well I was enrolling not at The Citadel but at the College of Charleston, where not only were local high school graduates charged no tuition but also there was no cadet corps with its accompanying rigors. But as for the possibility of any future military or naval involvement, when I thought about it at all I foresaw no problems. It seemed remote and hypothetical, something to be read about and imagined.*

Military activity in the area began to pick up well before Pearl Harbor. Uniforms were increasingly in evidence on the downtown streets, and newcomers were arriving in town to take the jobs that were opening up at the burgeoning defense installations north of the city. When news of the attack on Pearl Harbor came I was eighteen years old and a college sophomore. Thereafter new people thronged into the area, the waterfront was closed to visitors, rumors began circulating of ships being torpedoed and sunk off the coast by German U-boats, and as never before in living memory there was an abundance of folding money in Charleston. I found a summer job as a checker at the Port of Embarkation, paying $120 a month, which was notably better than the seven dollars a week I had earned the summer before as the sole reporter for a struggling weekly newspaper in North Charleston.

The awaited overnight metamorphosis in physique and in athletic skills had not yet occurred, nor did it do so when my family moved to Richmond and I switched to the University of Richmond that fall for my junior year. In late autumn, after I turned nineteen, I went downtown to take a physical examination for admission into the Marine Corps officers training program. I was turned down; it seemed that my chest expansion was insufficiently large.

*When in 1940 an older cousin in Richmond graduated from college he began taking flying lessons, with a view toward being admitted into the Army Air Corps. I asked him whether he was also considering the Navy's flight program. "No," he said. "I don't want anything having to do with an aircraft carrier." This struck me as quite theoretical, even a bit fanciful; any such eventuality seemed to lie far off in the future. Three years later he died when the P-38 he was flying as a squadron commander was shot down over Bremen, Germany.

After several months of working out with a medicine ball, I tried again, taking the train up to Washington for another examination, only to be told this time that my ears were too clogged with wax to be checked. I located a physician near the recruiting office, had my ears cleaned out, then returned to the examination. It was then discovered that I was partly color-blind. So back to Richmond I went. Not for a moment did it occur to me that the Marine Corps might have been trying to tell me something. A Navy officers training program was not an alternative, for I had never learned how to swim. So I decided to await my country's call via the Selective Service System.

In no way did any of this make a dent in my confidence. Just as I would assuredly wake up one morning to discover I was now ready for major-league baseball, so by the time my country summoned me I would have undergone swift transformation into a replica of Black Jack Pershing or Sergeant York.

Shortly before the end of the school year my country did call, and I spent most of the summer of 1943 as one of the more inept recruits ever to stumble through the Army's basic infantry training cycle at Fort McClellan, Alabama. Neither did this daunt me; I immediately applied for Officers Training School, and was swiftly rejected. Eventually I ended up at Fort Benning, Georgia, writing for the post newspaper.

Before that I spent six months in an Italian language program at Yale, where I barely managed to complete the course, followed by several dreary months as a casual at a largely unoccupied Army camp in northern New York State, awaiting reassignment.

From the latter, one memory stands out. I had been issued a pass and gone into Watertown, New York, to have dinner at a restaurant. It was a damp, misty evening—Lake Ontario was less than twenty-five miles distant—and except for the fact that it was not January or February but mid-April, seemed not unlike certain winter evenings in Charleston. Afterwards I went for a walk. In the darkness the houses and lawns, set back from the street, had a sequestered, withdrawn look to them. At one corner, in a grass plot across from an intersection, I came upon a monument illuminated by floodlights. Upon a pedestal, the frosted light falling unevenly on its metallic form, was the statue of a Union soldier. I was startled, taken aback. It seemed wrong, out of place.

In the bus on the way back to camp I thought about what I had seen, and my surprise upon catching sight of it. It was myself, not the Union soldier, who had been the one out of place. Yet was it only because I was there in a northern state, a long way from where I had grown up? Was it even because I was an enlisted man in the Army, engaged in an enterprise at which I was proving to be so poorly fitted and so self-evidently useless? If I were back in the South, in Charleston, would I have been fully at home even then? Had I ever been?

It was during those months, I believe, that I began to see things a bit differently. In any event, by the time the war was over and I returned to college for my senior year, I was prepared to recognize that whatever the glories of the Southern military tradition, such abilities as I possessed obviously did not lie in that direction.

So ended my career as a soldier. As the old Confederate is reported as having said, "I killed about as many of them as they did of me."

While in the Army I had for the first time in my life been in the everyday company of northerners and midwesterners, and had discovered that not all of my social and political assumptions were necessarily theirs. Sometimes there was much to be said for their way of viewing things. Yet the effect of the overall experience had been to reinforce my sense of being a southerner. At the same time, I was made more aware that to belong to a community carried not only the right but the obligation to examine its shortcomings as well as its virtues.

The realization that a typewriter keyboard was a more feasible mode of self-expression for me than a rifle, or for that matter a baseball, did not serve to lessen my interest in military history. If anything it facilitated it, because I could begin to concentrate my attention on what lay within my own range of competence. In intricate ways my own identity was involved in my relationship to the South, and clearly much of what had shaped the South was ingrained in its military history—which, however, I was learning to see was not necessarily an affair of good guys and bad guys.

What appealed to me most, as the 1940s became the 1950s, and could offer me the deepest and most vivid insights into the South and my ties with it, was the literature written by novelists and poets. That literature was drenched in history, and professionally I found that to move from one approach to the other was a matter of imaginative emphasis, not of kind. The Civil War, its causes, conduct, and consequences, was a useful component of both.

During those years the centennial anniversary of the Civil War was approaching. Refighting the war, always a popular intellectual pastime in the South, was shifting into high gear. The tourist industry began preparing eagerly for the coming bonanza, as did the book trade. The planned commemoration was expected to be a four-year-long affair of dedications, battlefield reenactments, and hands-across–Cemetery Ridge demonstrations, just as had happened at the fiftieth anniversary in 1913, although this time the actual wartime participants themselves would not be available to take part.

What was also happening, however, was that in the wake of the Second World War, black Americans were now demanding their basic rights as American citizens. The furor over public school desegregation, voting rights, and an end to second-class citizenship intensified. In reminding the nation why the war of 1861–1865 had been fought, the Civil Rights movement thoroughly undercut the assumption that the centennial would be no more than a vehicle for commemorative oratory.

The process was vividly illustrated in Charleston. In the late 1950s the centennial committees of the various states arranged for a planning meeting there where the war had commenced. When the New Jersey delegation arrived, it was discovered that its black members would not be allowed to stay at any of the leading hotels. The entire delegation promptly departed for home. In short, it was not going to be possible to ignore the connection between how the war was fought from why it was fought.

It should be emphasized that for all the denunciations, manifestos, courthouse rallies, school closings, expressions of editorial defiance, cross burnings, and, in a few instances in the Deep South, outright violence that disfigured the Southern scene in those years, a decided majority of leading Southern historians, as well as most of its better novelists and poets, fully supported the Civil Rights movement. For the most part it was not the South's scholars, authors, and educators, but its lawyers, evangelical preachers, and editors (though not its news reporters) who provided ideological rationale for the Dixiecrats, Citizens Councils, Defenders of State Sovereignty, and other champions of resistance to racial desegregation.

Even so, certain uncomfortable historical associations were in place, and with a moral edge to them that before the 1940s had not seemed as keen. If Pickett's Charge had broken the Union line along Cemetery Ridge and the road to Washington had been opened to Lee's army, would the result have been desirable or undesirable? If the latter, then how reconcile that with one's instinctive emotional loyalties?

Another and less ideological factor was impacting upon the reading and writing of Civil War military history in the 1950s and 1960s. As new book after book about the war was published, not only repetition but also outright duplication of topic and approach multiplied. More and more was being published about less and less. Some useful and informative books continued to be written, and certain facile assumptions and partisan interpretations received needed revision; but the ratio of heat to light grew ever more inefficient with each book-publishing season.

Not a few good Civil War historians began to examine the doings of generals and politicians of other wars and crises for possible study. Others took to repeating themselves. By the time the centennial years drew to an end, books on the Civil War were becoming a glut on the history market.

The outstanding work of military history to emerge from the centennial era was Shelby Foote's three-volume *The Civil War: A Narrative* (1958, 1963, 1974). In it, Foote was able to move beyond the resentments, rivalries, special pleadings, and biases of a century of sectional antagonism to provide a genuinely objective work of history. His was not another version, however well written, of the proverbial "non-partisan history of the War from the Southern point of view." I doubt that it could have been written any earlier than it was.

So far as I was concerned, Shelby's interpretation of the waging of the War Between the States was definitive. No major archives remained unexamined that might offer material for significant reassessment. There was and would always be room for further clarification of individual personalities and particular campaigns. A momentous change in historical attitudes was taking place, however, both because of the passage of time and because of the political, social, and economic developments that followed the Second World

War and paralleled the coming of the centennial. The Civil War, viewed as a sectional conflict, was no longer the decisive fact of Southern experience.

Add to that the unpleasant emotional associations that involved being on the wrong side of a moral issue, and for this particular reader the continued contemplation of the history of the War Between the States was over.

In recent years my own interest in military history has been centered upon the First World War. This is no new concern. Not only were my father and my uncles directly involved in that war, but Charleston and the South were basically an Anglophile community. As a reader of history I identified England's cause with our own— and, I continue to think, for good reason.

The Great War of 1914–1918 ushered in the world that I was born into and as I write this still inhabit. It was appropriate that the fighting on the Western Front ended with an armistice, because World War II was essentially a resumption of hostilities on an even more terrible scale, not a separate conflict. Historically there can be no question of the responsibility for war in 1939; it was a German and Japanese enterprise all the way. By contrast, the coming of war in 1914, the relative responsibility of the various European nations for its advent and spread, the reasons why those involved entered the conflict, even the tactics and strategy continue in dispute to this day. There remains a feeling of avoidability about the outbreak of the Great War, a sense that the descent into the abyss could have been averted. The discrepancy between its causes and its catastrophic results continues to seem appalling.

The generation of Americans who took part in the Great War were the grown-ups of my childhood and youth. During the decades after World War II they began leaving the scene in large numbers. There was a poignancy to the memory of their now-long-ago mustering-in and going forth to war that tugged at one's heartstrings, and the more so nowadays because the veterans of 1941–1945 are in their turn engaged in departing.

War is not to be sentimentalized, and in chronicling the ways of its waging there can be little place for nostalgia. Yet the account of those who have engaged in it is of people, not machines, and to seek to understand what they did and what prompted them to do it is as equally pertinent to the pursuit of human wisdom as any other kind of inquiry. Military history, as a record of human endeavor, is a chronicle of both good and evil, embodied in forms whose recurring patterns we may ignore or reject only to our own deprivation.

Since the day that I rode my bicycle down to the waterfront in hopes of seeing a fleeing ship arrive, just as one had in 1914, close to seven decades have gone by. During almost all that time I have lived in the Southeast, but elsewhere than in Charleston. Yet so far as my imagination goes I have never moved away. To that extent, I remain a product of the time and place I was born into, and my emotional and intellectual expectations have clearly been shaped in important ways by the loyalties and assumptions that came with the place where I grew up.

What makes individual human beings into what they become is a complicated matter, not to be explained by a simple formula of having been exposed to the ideals of a community. I concede that in a sense, given the set of needs that as a child and youth I brought to it, the impact of the community helped to formulate goals for me for which in key respects I was essentially unfitted, and that to a degree were even contradictory. It is possible that in a different milieu my ambition might have been directed toward objectives that were more compatible with what I had to offer, so that I might have been able to use such talents as I possessed to better effect than I have done. Yet the person who would have grown up under those different circumstances would have been someone other than myself.

Earlier I described my experiences, as a small child in the late 1920s, when witnessing a dress parade by The Citadel cadets. In the 1980s I was a guest of honor at a dress parade there. From the grandstand in front of the barracks I watched the cadet corps, now far larger than during my childhood, execute the same familiar maneuvers, lined up in company front, the cadet officers with red sashes and shining swords, rifles at shoulder arms and pennons flying. The principal guest that day was the vice president of a Latin American republic, who was clad in a resplendent white uniform with all manner of ribbons, medals, and brightly polished insignia, and who took the salute of the corps as it passed in review. I found the spectacle as enthralling as ever, in particular the cadet band, now augmented by a bagpipe corps clad in kilts, ninety-eight strong in all.

It struck me that in half a century I had done little more than move from one side of the field to the other—from my position with other neighborhood children and nurses at the edge of the parade ground next to Hampton Park, across to the reviewing stand. All was taking place as I recollected.

Yet there was one surprise awaiting me. This time, as if to remind me of my long-ago discomfort with the sunset gun, when the moment came for the lowering of the colors, instead of the single discharge from a field piece that I expected, no less than seven long-barreled cannon, firing seriatim, blasted out a nineteen-gun salute to the visiting Latin American dignitary. It was one crash after another, the noise reverberating off the surrounding gray buildings, the odor of burning powder, the thick cloud of yellow-white smoke drifting across the parade grounds and over into the treetops in Hampton Park, and as the tumult receded, the music of the ninety-eight-man band playing the National Anthem. The salvos of the guns that fired on Fort Sumter from the Battery and around the harbor could scarcely have been louder.

To the tune of the President's March, the drums and bagpipes alternating with the brass and reeds, the South Carolina Corps of Cadets paraded past the review stand and off the field. I was still a spectator, looking on admiringly at the soldiers.

2

The Summer the Archduke Died

(2002)

Now that blood will be redeemed for gold
Eagle and crown aglitter in the wheel,
In the summer, when the Archduke dies,
Europe divides and fuses, side by side

—*Howard Nemerov, "Sarajevo"*

After all these years there remains a fearful poignancy about the events that culminated in the outbreak of war in Europe in the summer of 1914. For thirty-seven days, from the slaying of the Archduke Franz Ferdinand and his wife at Sarajevo on June 28 until the German armies crossed the border into Belgium on August 3, the fate of the Western world lay in abeyance. After that, everything happened sequentially, as cause and effect. The history of our own times may be said to have begun.

What brought on the Great War, as it was generally called, and where the responsibility for its coming lay, continue to be as much the topic of historical dispute as ever. By contrast, the origins of

World War II, a far more lethal conflict, with fifty millions dead as against ten million, seem fairly straightforward. There is little or no sense of anyone's having blundered into war in 1939–1941. However belated or mistaken, the steps that nations took were deliberate. In 1914, on the other hand, none of the major participants realized what they were about to get into, much less where doing so was to take them.

The chasm between what those who chose to go to war thought that they could achieve, and the devastating consequences of their choice, is central to the continuing sense of regret. It is difficult to think of any benefits arising from what ensued that could compensate, whether in human life or in material advantage, for the losses incurred. Such gains as resulted not only could but very likely would have come on their own. The Great War need not and ought not have been fought.

A variety of explanations, whether metaphysical, psychological, biological, political, or economic, have been advanced to account for the onset of war in 1914. Exponents of the two most ubiquitous schools of popular social theorizing of the era, Social Darwinism and Marxism, had their proposed answers. The Marxists claimed that the war was the final stage of capitalistic exploitation, whereby the rival capitalist societies had begun killing off each other. The Social Darwinists proclaimed it the inevitable survival of the fittest, most vigorous and virile nation, or Empire, or *Volk*, or whatever. Neither theory—and the premises of both are remarkably similar—has aged very convincingly.

What they and most other such formulations share is the conviction that the outbreak of war in Europe was inevitable. Whether due to the nature of humankind or of the social units it has developed, whatever set the guns of August to roaring when and as they did was bound to happen, and could not have been avoided. But all such fatalistic generalizations seem dubious and sophistical: *post hoc, ergo propter hoc*, as the logicians have it. Was war also inevitable between the United States and the Soviet Union during the Cold War period? Not a few prophets thought so; it turned out not to be. Commenting on events on the Western Front in the summer of 1917, the British historian A. J. P. Taylor reminds us that "Only death is inevitable. Short of that nothing is inevitable until it happens, and everything is inevitable once it has happened. The historian deals with past events and therefore to him all history is inevitable. But these past events were once in the future and then they were not inevitable" ("War by Timetable," *From the Boer War to the Cold War,* 187).

The question that Tolstoy raised about the Napoleonic Wars in his second epilogue to *War and Peace* remains valid: to what extent, if any, are such massive undertakings brought about by individual leaders? If certain performers had not been present on the historical stage, or if they had performed otherwise than they did, would things have gone differently, and the ultimate results importantly changed?

In thinking about the causes of the Great War, and the relative importance of individual leadership in its coming, we need to keep in mind several distinctions. For one thing, the tensions and antagonisms that can produce war among nations need not necessarily result in it. In the decades prior to 1914, Great Britain and Tsarist Russia, for example, were repeatedly at sword's point over their rivalry in India and Persia. War might have erupted there rather than along the border between Austria-Hungary and Serbia, which if it became general would surely have produced a different alignment of protagonists.

It is important, too, to distinguish between a local or regional war on the one hand, and European-wide or global war on the other. There was considerable historical precedent—1854, 1859, 1866, 1870 —for the former taking place without the latter being a necessary outcome. It is clear that in 1914 Austria-Hungary wanted a local war against Serbia, and that Germany was encouraging its ally to wage it. No nation, however, not even Germany, and certainly not Austria-Hungary, desired a full-scale, European-wide war.

This is not to say, of course, that in 1914 as in 1939 there were not individuals and even factions within Germany who were certain that it was their country's destiny to rule Europe and who looked forward to the war that was to bring that about. Nor that within Germany as well as elsewhere in those years, there were not those who wrote and believed that war was the test of a people's true worthiness, a cleansing and purifying antidote to the materialistic pleasuring of a European society that had grown effete and self-indulgent.

Neither Kaiser Wilhelm II nor any other heads of government, how-ever, deliberately sought to bring about the European immolation that came.

What Germany was willing to do, and what finally resulted in the war, was to *risk* the possibility of full-fledged war in order to achieve its objectives. When word came of the assassination of the Archduke, Kaiser Wilhelm II promptly extended his famous "blank check" to Austria-Hungary: proceed against the Serbs, and if Russia (and its ally France) attempts to interfere, an attack on you will be consid-ered an attack on Germany. As for Austria-Hungary, once it had Ger-many's assurance of help it too would accept the risk of a major war. Russia for its part, rather than let Serbia go under and its own influ-ence in southern Europe and the Balkans be eroded, would accept the risk of war, provided France would join in. France in turn would go to war if Russia were attacked, preferring to fight in company with an ally to a future conflict in which it might have to face a vic-torious Germany alone. The threat and risk of a major war was thus allowed to become a tool of diplomatic maneuver.

Before 1914 there had been a series of crises in which war between the major European powers appeared possible. On each occasion the result had been compromise, with both sides backing off, but with the cumulative result that an ultimate shoot-out seemed ever more unavoidable. In Germany, which saw its ally Austria-Hungary's strength and prestige steadily waning even while Russia's military capabilities were swiftly recovering from the defeat by Japan in 1904–1905, there was growing talk of fighting a preventive war while the odds were still in its favor.

Even so, the alacrity with which Imperial Germany and its ally Austria-Hungary were willing to risk full-scale war following the murder of the Archduke and his wife at Sarajevo is striking. In Aus-tria-Hungary's instance, to be sure, there were reasons having to do with internal politics. The Dual Monarchy was experiencing repeat-ed trouble among the sizable Slavic nationalist elements within its polyglot population; by crushing Serbia it could suppress the single most active external encouragement for such agitation—so long as German support could be counted on to forestall intervention by Russia. But in Samuel R. Williamson's words, "The danger lay in seeking to resolve a domestic issue by a foreign policy adventure, since almost no one ever considered alleviating a foreign policy problem by domestic reform" (*Austria-Hungary and the Origins of the First World War,* 11).

Germany likewise had internal problems to deal with: vexatious labor troubles, a semi-feudal Prussian governmental structure under increasing fire from the sizable socialist representation in the Reichstag, and a burgeoning middle-class population demanding a greater voice and role in government. Yet whatever might be true for Austria-Hungary, the Kaiser's regime scarcely faced a comparable threat from within, and it would be misleading to say that the Reich's foreign policy was in any crucial way a response to internal political pressures. Of more import was the military leadership's growing unease over the prospect of having to fight on both Eastern and Western fronts. In 1912, as Hew Strachan points in the impressive first volume of his new overall history of the Great War, the German chief of staff, Helmuth von Moltke the younger, was declaring that "war was inevitable, and the sooner it came the better for Germany" (*The First World War: Volume I: To Arms,* 52). A month before Sarajevo, Moltke warned the German foreign minister, Gottlieb von Jagow, that "we must wage a preventive war to conquer our opponents as long as we still have a reasonable chance in this struggle" (63).

Beyond doubt, in all of Imperial Germany's performances on the world scene following the enforced retirement of Otto von Bismarck in 1889 there was a decided element of sheer nationalistic vaunting. The unification of Germany in 1870, together with the Reich's formidable growth and expanding prosperity, threw the European balance of power into disarray. Within the matter of a few decades Germany had become the European continent's foremost industrial and military power. Its leadership, from its blustering Kaiser on down, and, indeed, no small segment of its flourishing population wanted that superior status acknowledged, and the tactics employed to secure such acknowledgment were in no way subtle. The result was that, in Andreas Hillgruber's formulation, "Public opinion in other European nations slowly came to sense a threat, less because of the goals of German foreign policy per se than the crude, overbearing style that Germany projected on the international stage" (*Germany and the Two World Wars,* 9).

The equilibrium was rendered all the more unstable by the exposed volatility of the "powder keg of Europe," the Balkans, where the Ottoman Empire was in the late stages of disintegration. In scarcely more than a year's time there were two Balkan wars. Not only were the various small nations which had for centuries constituted Turkey's European provinces rivals for contested territory and populations, but Austria-Hungary had its designs and ambitions for the region, as did Tsarist Russia. German commercial interests were likewise flourishing in Asia Minor, and the railroad route to Baghdad led through the Balkan peninsula. In what seemed the likely event of the total elimination of what still remained of Ottoman domain in Europe, possession of Constantinople and control of the Straits became of vital concern.

The major European powers had developed a series of alliances and ententes, the composition of which fluctuated somewhat but by the early 1900s had evolved into a Triple Alliance made up of Germany, Austria-Hungary, and Italy, as against a similar defensive pact between France and Russia. As the threat of war surfaced, Great Britain drew closer to France and Russia, to the extent of making joint war plans in case France was attacked by Germany and agreeing to hold naval conversations with Russia; no formal commitments, however, were signed. Italy, which if a major power at all was clearly the weakest one, meanwhile showed signs of unwillingness to be tied to the support of its allies in the event of fighting.

Supposedly designed to preserve peace by preventing any one nation from daring to attack another, the alliances if anything turned out to facilitate the opposite result, for by broadening the likely scope of a war and raising the stakes, they intensified the collective insecurity. When the crisis of 1914 came, there was a kind of chain reaction, the culmination of a gathering tension that during the preceding decade had encouraged a growing fatalism about the probability of war.

An obvious outcome of the pervading unease was the urgent need on all sides for expanded military expenditures, and this in an era when scientific and industrial advances in weaponry and equipment were making the tools of warfare considerably more lethal than ever before. Smokeless powder, bolt-action magazine rifles, machine guns, rapid-firing artillery accurate over long distances, explosives of far greater destructiveness, railroad networks for swift movement of troops and supplies, the beginnings of air power, at sea the development of powerful battle fleets and the introduction of submarines, all demanded the steady enlargement of European military budgets.

Expanding populations, more numerous and prosperous middle classes, and developing industrial proletariats were opening up additional revenue opportunities for European governments to pay for these costly new weapons. With these, however, came widespread demands for larger outlays for education and social services, and resentment of the old landowning class's hitherto largely sacrosanct monopoly of government offices, legislative representation and influence, and the opportunity for military careers—and thus more fiscal stress and internal dispute. There can be no question that one way of countering the intensity of such protest was to encourage chauvinistic nationalism and to stress military and naval perils.

As each nation's armed forces developed their new weaponry and planned their strategies, the natural impatience of military men with the compromises and maneuverings of politicians was accompanied by an equally natural professional eagerness to take to the offensive. Evidence that the long-familiar Napoleonic tactics of attack had been rendered dangerously obsolete by machine guns, rapid-firing rifles, and massed long-range artillery tended to be discounted by the high commands of the various armies. Instead, the assumption was widespread that through superior élan and patriotism, each nation's forces would carry the day in what all but the most pessimistic assumed would surely be a brief but decisive war.

Of the personalities who were active on the European scene during the years when the Great War was in the offing, by all odds the most prominent—and the most erratic—was Kaiser Wilhelm II. From his ascent to the Imperial throne in 1888 onward, Wilhelm rattled the saber often and noisily, extolled and encouraged German militarism, and took the lead in creating and expanding the High Seas Fleet, the last not only converting Great Britain from a friend to an adversary but thoroughly stimulating anti-English prejudice within his own constituency as a way of winning approval for the formidable expenditure required.

Yet some who knew him best believed that, though scarcely a calming presence on the European scene, Wilhelm didn't really want war, and certainly not against England, so much as the gilt and panoply that went along with German martial prominence. What he liked was dressing up in a uniform and making bellicose speeches. On the day war was declared, France's ambassador to Germany, Jules Cambon, remarked to the English ambassador, Sir Edward Goschen, that only three persons in Berlin were unhappy about its coming—the two of them and the Kaiser. "It was his own and our misfortune," his onetime chancellor, Bernhard von Bülow, wrote in retrospect, "that his words and his gestures never coincided with his real attitude in the matter. When he boasted or even threatened people in words, it was often because he wanted to allay his own timidity" (John Van der Kiste, *Kaiser Wilhelm II*, 170–71).

Even though the Kaiser's word was supposedly law, with the leadership theoretically answerable to him and not to any legislative body, most students of Wilhelmine German policy have come to depict the Emperor as more manipulated than manipulating. There can be no question, however, that Wilhelm, even though maneuvered by others, contributed greatly in helping to establish a frame of mind, both in Germany and among its neighbors, whereby war seemed an acceptable expedient. In effect, he was trapped within his own belligerent stance, and never more so than when he extended the famous "blank check" to Austria-Hungary. That was the decision that most of all assured the coming of war in 1914, although at the last minute Wilhelm and Chancellor Theobald von Bethmann Hollweg sought briefly to draw back.

Certainly the responsibility for the outbreak of the First World War cannot be assigned solely to Germany. Yet it seems likely that if there had been no aggressive, expansionist Imperial Germany on the European scene in the early years of the twentieth century, there might have been local wars, but not the international conflagration that burst forth in 1914. In assuring Austria-Hungary of unqualified support for whatever punitive action it took against Serbia, the German high command was fully aware that Russia might mobilize in defense of its fellow Slavs, and that a war with Russia would also mean war with its ally France and quite likely with England. Germany was willing, to an extent even eager, to risk the confrontation. The rationale of the military leadership was, as already noted, Better Sooner Than Later.

The Schlieffen Plan which prescribed the Kaiser's army's response to the coming of war, as modified by Moltke, was based on the premise that Germany must above all avoid having to sustain an extended two-front war. The essence of the plan was swiftness. Within six weeks German armies were to strike through neutral Belgium at the French flank, encircle and crush French resistance, and occupy Paris. The bulk of the fighting forces could then be speedily transferred eastward by rail to handle the oncoming but slowly moving Russians.

What distinguished Germany's mobilization plan from those of the other major continental powers was that it involved not only preparations for attack but also the commission of an actual act of war. There was little or no place for flexibility in the German response. To open up a pathway through Belgium before the French could shift troops northward to counter the attack, each of four German armies, upon arriving at the rail junction at Aachen where several lines converged, was to move on into Luxembourg and across the Belgian border, thus making room for the next arrivals.

Immediately following the Russian order to begin mobilization, Germany would issue an ultimatum, and when it was rejected would declare war. Ultimatums would be delivered to Belgium and France, and upon their rejection the invasion would begin. (In the unlikely event that the French replied by saying that they had no intention to begin mobilization, they would be required to demonstrate good faith by surrendering control of several key border forts.) As for what action the British were likely to take, if, as was expected, England did come to Belgium's and France's aid, its small army would not be a deterrent. Once set in motion the elaborate German timetable could not be altered.

There is some doubt whether Kaiser Wilhelm II understood that his high command's plans required the perpetration of an act of war, one that was almost certain to ensure that Great Britain would enter the conflict, or in any event whether he grasped its full implications. It is not even certain that the Kaiser had been informed of what his high command's mobilization plans entailed. "If only someone had told me beforehand that England would take up arms against us," he declared in later years. Barbara Tuchman, in *The Guns of August* (1962), is skeptical about the Kaiser's lament, as are many others. Yet such was Wilhelm's notorious penchant for seeing only what he wished to see that England's probable course may indeed have been unclear to him. Depending upon which way the wind might appear to be blowing, the Kaiser could reverse judgments and draw new conclusions almost hourly.

Reichschancellor Bethmann Hollweg knew what the Schlieffen Plan involved, however, and several days prior to the commencement of hostilities he actually proposed to the English ambassador in Berlin that if Britain would agree to stay out, Germany would honor Dutch, but not Belgian, neutrality and maintain French territorial integrity, though without making any guarantees about France's overseas possessions. The crudeness of the proposal, which was not only unacceptable but a dead giveaway to what Germany planned to do, is all too emblematic of the appalling insensitivity that characterized Imperial Germany's dealing with other nations throughout its brief forty-eight-year history.

It has been customary among historians to fault the British government and its foreign minister, Sir Edward Grey, for failing to deliver an unmistakable message in 1914 that if France was threatened by Germany, England would go to its rescue. Yet Great Britain had demonstrated the likelihood of that response at Tangier in 1905 and again at Agadir in 1911. On several occasions the German leadership had been warned that Britain would not consent to having control of the continent of Europe, including the North Sea and Channel ports, seized by a single dominant power, and the more so because Germany now possessed a battle fleet second only to England's in size and strength. As recently as 1912 Britain had made it clear that however desirable a naval agreement and an easing of the Anglo-German naval race might be, it was not willing to secure it at the price of pledging neutrality if an attack were made on France.

Whatever may have been the myopia and/or wishful thinking of the Kaiser and his political leaders, the high command of the German army knew very well what Britain would do, and it was in no way deterred. Moltke himself is said to have had private doubts of his army's invincibility, but, as noted, he favored going ahead while the odds were in Germany's favor. He was convinced that on the high seas the Kaiser's vaunted navy, which wanted to postpone the fatal step, would never pronounce itself ready to take on the British fleet, while on land Russia's army was growing stronger with each passing year. In the words of Bethmann Hollweg in 1918, "Yes, My God, in a certain sense it was a preventive war. But when war was hanging above us, when it had to come in two more years even more dangerously and more inescapably, and when the generals said, now it is still possible, without defeat, but not in two years time. Yes, the generals!" (quoted in Immanuel Geiss, "The Outbreak of the First World War and German War Aims," in Walter Laqueur and George L. Mosse, eds., *1914: the Coming of the First World War*, 78).

The fatalism that had permeated German thinking about the inevitability of war by the time of the assassination of the Archduke Franz Ferdinand, therefore, meant that, while hoping to restrict its ally's chastisement of Serbia to a localized punitive action, the Reich's leadership was willing to take the very real chance that it might well have to redeem its "blank check" with full-fledged war against Russia and France. In the wake of Sarajevo, sympathy for Austria-Hungary was widespread throughout Europe, and a strong ultimatum to Serbia, one that would administer a severe humiliation to that country but stop short of war, might well have been acceptable even to Russia. Not until too late in the accelerating crisis, however, and after Austria-Hungary had begun hostilities, did the Kaiser's government make a serious attempt to restrain its ally. Even then, when Britain proposed an international meeting by the major powers, Germany would not go along. And when at the last minute Bethmann Hollweg sought to persuade Austria-Hungary to halt its army at Belgrade, Moltke was advising it to begin mobilization against Russia.

Tsarist Russia's part in the coming of war, to be sure, was not that of an innocent bystander. As protector of the southern Slavs, a role assumed in part to divert attention from its own severe political and economic problems, it had been unable to block Austria-Hungary's annexation of Bosnia and Herzegovina in 1908, and its authority and prestige in the Balkans, where it had ambitions, were at issue now. While Russia would have preferred a diplomatic solution to the crisis, it would not countenance Serbia being so weakened as to make Austria-Hungary and Germany dominant in the region, and for Serbia to be decisively beaten militarily would jeopardize long-range Russian ambitions to control Constantinople and achieve unchallenged access to the Mediterranean.

So the Tsar's government encouraged Serbia not to accept any punitive conditions that would importantly infringe upon its independence, and when the long-delayed Austro-Hungarian ultimatum did arrive, with several of its provisions obviously designed to be unacceptable, it was followed the next day by a decision in Russia to begin partial mobilization. The Tsar's military leadership, however, at once pressed for full mobilization, arguing that to mobilize only in those districts confronting Austria-Hungary would so disrupt the timetables that if it then became necessary to muster against Germany as well, the defense of Russia would be gravely endangered.

As for Germany, its political leadership, confident of their army's superior military preparations and skills, was willing to hold off until the Russians actually ordered mobilization, believing that the swiftness and efficiency with which Germany's mobilization plans could proceed would make up for a late start. Everything possible must be done to forestall Great Britain from coming to the aid of France and Russia, and the best way to manage that, given the known reluctance of influential elements of the British government to become involved in a European war of any kind, would be to appear to be responding to Russian mobilization rather than making the first move. Indeed, as Marc Trachtenberg writes, "they would have been delighted if, after mobilization, France had been the first to attack" ("The Meaning of Mobilization in 1914," in Steven E. Miller et al., *Military Strategy and the Origins of the First World War*, 222).

Tsar Nicholas II held off for five days before capitulating to the demand by his generals for full mobilization. Partial Russian mobilization, however, was sufficient to alarm the German high command, and preliminary steps for mobilization were also taken. Once the Tsar gave in and full mobilization was decreed, the German high command ordered its own mobilization to begin. Inasmuch as that would entail actually moving across the border into Belgium, war was made inevitable.

While France's political leadership hoped to avoid any war at all, any hedging on its ties with Russia might at a future date leave an isolated France exposed to a militant Germany that would no longer be hampered by the constraints of a two-front war. So it did not exert pressure upon its ally to acquiesce either in a negotiated Austro-Serbian settlement or a restricted Austrian punitive action. The French army itself, however, was given strict instructions to pull back ten kilometers from the German border and under no circumstances to shoot first; to do otherwise might jeopardize British support.

The German hope that if war with France and Russia came Great Britain might not join its enemies arose, as noted earlier, not from any concern over a possible participation of the small British army in the effort to impede its planned sweep through Belgium and northern France; what the Kaiser's government feared was the Royal Navy. German merchant ships would be driven from the seas, German colonies in Africa and Asia would be captured, and a naval blockade would deny imports of munitions and food to Germany and its ally Austria-Hungary, while making them abundantly available to their opponents. Even if the French armies were routed according to plan and the Tsar's armies pushed far back onto the steppes of central Russia, there was no guarantee that British seapower would relax its naval grip.

When following the violation of Belgium's borders the British government issued its ultimatum to Germany, the Kaiser was outraged at what he considered an act of betrayal. His mother was English, his grandmother was Queen Victoria; he considered himself a true friend of Britain. This despite the fact that from the time of his accession to the throne onward, he had not hesitated, in seeking support for the High Seas Fleet he so coveted, to play up to the Anglophobia that increasingly characterized German public opinion.

Granted the Kaiser's well-known instability and subjectivity, it is possible to credit the sincerity, however erratic, of his earlier vehement denials whenever anyone ventured to suggest that the creation of a German battle fleet when none had existed before was intended as a challenge to the Royal Navy. As Lamar Cecil notes in his biography of the Kaiser, apparently Wilhelm II genuinely believed that Germany could pursue the simultaneous goals of increasing the size of its battle fleet and reaching a naval accommodation with Britain (*Wilhelm II: Emperor and Exile, 1900–1941*, 333).

Admiral Alfred von Tirpitz knew better, and it was he who kept the course of the German High Seas Fleet resolutely pointed toward what for him was a necessary ultimate confrontation with the eventual enemy. Using his astute political talents, he manipulated popular dislike of England so that the fleet was made into the rallying emblem of national expansion and imperial ambition.

As several Reichschancellors phrased it in turn, Germany required its rightful "place in the sun," and there was general agreement that it was mainly England, with her empire and her navy, that was blocking the way. Each successive international incident—the Morocco crisis, Bosnia-Herzegovina, the Kaiser's *Daily Telegraph* interview, the *Panther* confrontation—intensified the German popular resentment. "It is false that in Germany the nation is peaceful and the government bellicose—the exact opposite is true," the French ambassador to Berlin, Jules Cambon, reported to Paris in 1911 (Konrad H. Jarausch, *The Enigmatic Chancellor: Bethmann Hollweg and the Hubris of Imperial Germany*, 124).

One can understand Germany's behavior in 1914, it has been argued, if one keeps in mind the dread of hostile encirclement felt by the Reich as it observed Austria-Hungary's spreading governmental paralysis and Italy's drift away from commitment to the Triple Alliance, even as Russia was enlarging its armies and its rail network and France was extending its two-year military service law by an additional year. If to those developments were added the naval might and vast resources of the British Empire, Germany would be endangered indeed. It was something of a self-fulfilling prognosis. As Hew Strachan phrases it, "The fear which had accompanied German assertiveness gained the upper hand: the bull in the china-shop of European diplomacy began to see itself as a resigned sacrificial victim" (62).

The menace of any such encirclement was mainly self-induced. The wars of German unification, followed by Wilhelm II's rhetoric, successive Naval Laws, *Weltpolitik*, and repeated brinkmanship had frightened France, Russia, and then England into mutual support and furnished the primary unsettling element in an increasingly volatile assemblage of European nation-states. And it must be said that the bombast and bravado of the Kaiser eerily mirrored the attitude of middle-class Germany. As Bethmann Hollweg himself remarked to Jules Cambon, "Don't you think that there is a public opinion in Germany which is easy to inflame in questions in which patriotism and self-interest combine? At any rate be fair enough to admit that I seek to arouse it as little as I try to follow it." Yet Bethmann too, as his biographer Konrad Jarausch readily concedes, "was spellbound by the glittering image of *Weltpolitik*, even if he pursued it with more moderate means" (145).

Was the Kaiser's Reich what I recall my history professor at the University of Richmond, R. C. McDanel, once saying: "Hitler's Germany with better manners"? Beyond question there was more continuity between the two Reichs than its own historians were for many years willing to admit. The Kaiser's Germany was permeated by a passionate nationalism, fueled by chauvinistic fervor and encouraged by hitherto-uninterrupted military success, which when thwarted and disappointed could and did become readily capable of exploding in resentment, the urge for revenge, and violent aggression.

The novelist Thomas Mann, who in 1914 thought the prospect of war an ennobling, purifying element (he was not alone), had by the time he wrote *The Magic Mountain* (1924) come to recognize the advent of the Great War for what it was: the confirmation of a terrible soul-sickness. In the climax of that novel, early in the twentieth century the patients in a Swiss Alpine sanatorium attend a séance, at which, through the demonaic artistry of a sorcerer and the conjuring-up of a collective prophetic apparition, they are made to confront the prophetic image of a soldier clad in a strange, field-gray uniform and wearing a steel helmet.

What happened to Germany, and plunged Europe and the world into war, was a catastrophic failure of statecraft, a collapse of leadership. It is difficult to quarrel with John C. G. Röhl's estimate ("Germany," in Keith Wilson ed., *Decisions for War, 1914*, 27):

> The leaders of arguably the most successful country in Europe, a country bursting with energy, boasting a young and dynamic population and an economy second to none, a country whose army, whose administration, whose scientific and artistic achievements were the envy of the world, took decisions which plunged it and the other powers into a ghastly war in which almost ten million men lost their lives, the old internal and international order was for ever destroyed, and popular hatreds were released which were to poison public life for generations to come.

3

"The Weasel's Twist, The Weasel's Tooth"

The First World War as Military History

(1995)

My favorite book in my very early teens was Floyd Gibbons's *The Red Knight of Germany,* a biography of Baron Manfred von Richthofen, who shot down eighty Allied airplanes before his own turn came. I had already begun reading all the books I could find about the First World War, beginning at age nine or ten with an affair entitled *Army Boys in French Trenches.* There was also a novel for boys involving some youthful British sailors aboard a gunboat or destroyer named something like the *Sylph,* and climaxing, I think, with the sinking of the German commerce raider *Emden* by the Australian cruiser *Sydney.* By comparison with those, my discovery of Floyd Gibbons's biography of Richthofen represented a step forward in sophistication and authenticity; after all, it was nonfiction, and it quoted from actual documents and reports.

Needless to say, the depiction of that conflict in such books differed sharply from that in the works of literature I began reading in college and thereafter. Offhand I can't recall a single important novel or poem about 1914–1918 that deals with the war as anything other than a bloodbath, which indeed it was. Its violent impact upon

British writers, both as it was taking place and later, has been sorted out and interpreted authoritatively by Samuel L. Hynes in *A War Imagined: The First World War and English Culture* (1990). Before that, Paul Fussell, in *The Great War and Modern Memory* (1975), developed a largely convincing thesis that the trauma of World War I had imprinted fundamental patterns upon the way we thought and viewed our experience.

My concern here, however, is not with the effects, psychological or aesthetic, of the First World War on literature, but with the way the war has been presented as military history. For every book that has been published about 1914–1918, there have probably been five on World War II. Between Armistice Day in 1918 and the Nazi invasion of Poland in 1939, barely two decades elapsed, and once the Second World War came along, few general readers wanted to read about its predecessor, so that not many new works of other than a scholarly nature were published on the 1914–1918 fracas. With a few notable exceptions this has continued to be true.*

There are understandable reasons for it. In the first place, nothing was really settled by all the carnage of World War I; the outbreak of World War II two decades later was not so much the start of a new war as a recommencement of the previous one. True, the First World War caused, or in any event hastened, the breakdown of Tsarist Russia and the advent of the Soviet Union, and it brought an end to the Austro-Hungarian Empire. But the central issue of the fighting in 1939 when the Germans invaded Poland and Britain and France declared war remained the same as it had been in 1914: whether or not Germany was to rule Europe and become the dominant power in the Western world. Not until 1944–1945 was the question settled and the German armed forces defeated on German soil and made to surrender unconditionally.

So a work of history that set out to interpret the First World War could offer its reader no real conclusion other than a chronological one, and to that extent it was deficient in dramatic resolution—a beginning, a middle, but no end. In effect, it was the nonfiction equivalent of a "slice of life" novel—more accurately, perhaps, slice of

*This essay was written in 1995; since then some excellent books on the military history of the First World War have appeared, among them the first volume, *To Arms,* of Hew Strachan's projected multivolume history, *The First World War* (New York, 2001).

death. Moreover, the individual military episodes had a sodden sameness about them. Unlike the Second World War, which was largely a war of movement, the War of 1914-1918 was mainly one in which the principal antagonists stayed in place and butted heads together. In the fast-developing campaigns of World War II, decisiveness, strategic imagination, and innovative leadership were important to what happened. On the Western Front in 1914–1918 this wasn't so.

Consider, for example, the fascination with the aerial aces of World War I, which exists even today. Only the other evening I watched a television documentary on the Red Baron. This fascination was understandable, because fighting between aircraft was almost the only kind of combat in 1914–1918 in which what individual human beings did could be singled out, and particular warriors identified as heroes. Who were the commanders in charge of the various components of the offense and defense at Passchendaele, the Somme, Verdun? Does it matter?

By contrast, the leading army commanders in World War II were recognizable personalities. The campaigns they directed were distinguishable from one another, their outcome attributable in important respects to the quality of leadership. Not even on the Eastern Front was the strategy basically that of attrition. This was true at sea as well; unlike Jutland in 1916, the naval battles of Coral Sea, Midway, and Leyte Gulf in the Pacific in 1941–1945 were decisive. Nor was there any difficulty in identifying the villains, for unlike what took place in the summer when the Archduke died, neither Germany nor Japan stumbled into war. On the contrary, they deliberately began it, were ruthless in their treatment of conquered territory and conquered peoples, and there could be no question about whether the rest of the civilized world would be better or worse off if the Axis Powers were to win.

For these reasons and others, then, the conduct of World War I has not been exactly a flourishing topic either for sustained historical analysis or for popular recapitulation. The best books about it have tended to be those which have sought to show how and why the war was allowed to happen. They make for melancholy reading, describing as they do the coming of a calamity that nobody wanted to happen, that could and should have been arrested, and that brought an end to an era in which the overall well-being of the citizenry of

Western Europe was probably at a higher level than ever before in history. Each time we read it, no matter how familiar the events chronicled, there is the sense of helplessness and futility, the instinctive hope and wish that long-since-happened history somehow won't happen. Henry James's famous comment to Howard Sturgis after war came was and is to the point: "The plunge of civilization into this abyss of blood and darkness by the wanton fear of those two infamous autocrats is a thing that so gives away the long age during which we have supposed the world to be, with whatever abatement, gradually bettering, that to have to take it all now for what the treacherous years were all the while really making for and meaning is too tragic for any words" (*Letters of Henry James*, edited by Percy Lubbock, II, 382).

Assuredly those in command—and also those who patriotically accepted their leadership—had no idea of just how dreadful modern warfare could be. What the high command in Germany and Austria-Hungary—along with some of the military leadership in Russia, France, Great Britain, and Italy—did want, and expected, was something brief and exciting, along the lines of the Franco-Prussian War. Another literary reference, this time from Yeats's "Nineteen Hundred and Nineteen," is appropriate:

> Parliament and king
> Thought that unless a little powder burned
> The trumpeters might burst with trumpeting
> And yet it lack all glory; and perchance
> The guardsmen's drowsy chargers would not prance.

The result was the hideous trench warfare of the Western Front, which Yeats's poem aptly characterized:

> We, who seven years ago
> Talked of honour and of truth,
> Shriek with pleasure if we show
> The weasel's twist, the weasel's tooth.

As for what happened to the human beings who made up the various armies once the fighting began, and who after a few months' time found themselves engaged in a warfare of attrition that was as monstrous and impersonal as it was unexpected, books of military history on the First World War have tended to be of two kinds. There have been military studies, which chronicle and analyze the events of the war in terms of the strategy and tactics used, and which are written by professional military historians, usually with military training. There have been more general works that concentrate upon showing just how terrible and futile was the mass slaughter of a conflict in which modern weaponry had rendered traditional methods of attack and breakthrough obsolete, yet the generals in charge seemed to know nothing better than to keep trying to use them.

While I do not claim to have read all the overall histories, I am familiar with a good many of them, and it seems to me that by and large this division still holds true. It is with this in mind that I want to comment on a new and I think very good book, *The First World War: A Complete History* (1995), by Martin Gilbert.

Gilbert, who is well known for the multivolumed biography of Winston Churchill—he took over after Randolph Churchill died and wrote six of the eight volumes—has centered his story on the officers and men in the ranks, describing what happened to numerous individual soldiers during the course of the various battles and campaigns. He states his intentions very clearly, and in his closing two sentences reiterates what he has been after: "All wars end up being reduced to statistics, strategies, debates about their origins and results. These debates about war are important, but not more important than the human story of those who fought in them" (543).

To illustrate what this approach means for Gilbert's book, let me cite an example. For the first day of the Battle of the Somme, July 1, 1916, we are given three-and-a-half pages of narrative, taking up the following items, in the order cited:

1. A song sung by British troops as they moved into position.

2. A poem written by a twenty-three-year-old participant in anticipation of the attack.

3. The preparatory artillery barrage.

4. The bulky, heavy equipment toted by the attackers, and two comments on its cumbersomeness.

5. The heroic action of a Scottish drummer in beating the charge and rallying the troops.

6. A lance corporal's description of men being mowed down by machine-gun fire.

7. German machine guns in action, and their lethalness.

8. A passage from a lieutenant's letter home, telling of the Germans he had killed, describing how Germans fired upon his men until about to be overrun and then attempted to surrender, how most of them were not allowed to do so but were killed, how some Germans had allowed British soldiers to dress their wounds and then shot them in the back: "They are swine—take it from me—I saw these things happen with my own eyes" (259).

9. Another lieutenant's description of a German soldier surrendering and begging for mercy—and apparently receiving it.

10. A medical officer's description of a man suffering from shell shock.

11. A lieutenant's successful efforts to get his men to follow him over the top, his leading them into No-Man's-Land, his being hit, being unable to keep going, taking refuge in a shell hole, crawling back to the British trenches and en route seeing "the hand of a man who'd been killed only that morning beginning to turn green and yellow. That made me pretty sick and I put on a spurt" (260).

12. The capture of two German-held villages, and the figures on British casualties during the first day's fighting—more than 21,000 killed, and 25,000 seriously wounded.

13. The killing of 159 men by a single German machine gun, their burial in a trench, and the notice put over their grave: "The Devonshires held this trench. The Devonshires hold it still" (260). Among them was the lieutenant whose poem was noted earlier.

14. What happened to another battalion, 520 of whose 836 men were killed and 316 wounded, with lines from an unfinished poem by one of the dead, and what an official historian later wrote of the action.

15. A sergeant who was hit and went back for medical help, returned to the front line to rescue a soldier unable to make it back on his own, and was thereafter never again seen. This is followed by seven lines of a poem he had written entitled "A Soldier's Funeral."

16. The sergeant's brother's description of the dying and wounded at a dressing station.

17. A Newfoundland battalion that was almost totally wiped out, and a quotation from a divisional commander praising their valor.

18. The loss of more than 500 attackers taken prisoner, and the failure of the assault to reach an objective located less than ten miles from the starting point.

In closing, we learn that the British attack did force the Germans to give up trying to capture Verdun from the French, and also that a French attack that same day, though making larger gains than the British, failed of its objective but took 3,000 prisoners and captured 80 German artillery pieces.

The handling of the first day of the Somme is representative of Gilbert's approach throughout. Particularly for the Western Front fighting, almost every important campaign is similarly depicted, though not usually at such length. No one can complain that in his treatment of the opening of the Somme offensive, Gilbert has not given ample attention to the "human story of those who fought" in that battle of eighty summers ago.

It is interesting to compare Gilbert's version of what was happening on the Somme with that in another useful but very different one-volume history of about the same length, *The Great War, 1914–1918* (1959), by Cyril Falls, a British military historian who fought in World War I. Falls devotes less than a page to the actual fighting, concentrating on the preparation and the results. One of his announced objectives in writing his book was to refute the myth, as he calls it, that "the military art stood still in the greatest war up to date" (10), and that its commanding generals were unimaginative elders who knew nothing better than to send masses of men over the top to get slaughtered.

Falls makes no criticism of Douglas Haig at the Somme, saying only that the British commander "must have been terribly disappointed that night" following the first day's fighting, but that "he was not yet aware of the terrible total of his losses" (201). Later he declares that, no longer expecting a breakthrough then and there, "Haig had gone over to *la guerre d'usure,* the warfare of attrition," and: "So it went on, Haig imperturbable and nursing the hope that by mid-September the German resistance would be so reduced that a powerful assault might lead to a break-through" (202).

Martin Gilbert's quite different view of Haig would appear to reflect his experience in writing the biography of Winston Churchill. He shares Churchill's distrust of the military leadership and abhorrence of its willingness to expend lives in fruitless Western Front offensives. Gilbert quotes Churchill's comment about the high command in a letter to an officer friend at the end of 1917: "Thank God our offensives are at an end. Let them traipse across the crater fields. Let them rejoice in the occasional capture of placeless names and sterile ridges" (389). In Gilbert's book, Haig comes across as a military mandarin who throughout the war kept insisting that the German army was on the brink of collapse and who ordered offensive after offensive, each time trading huge casualty lists for what proved to be insignificant gains. The date of Haig's accession to command of the British Expeditionary Force in place of Sir John French, December 19, 1915, which was also the day when the Germans first employed phosgene gas against the British, is characterized by Gilbert as "an ominous day for millions" (216).

The point is that Gilbert's approach to World War I, written by a man who is not a military historian as such, is concerned above all with showing its hideousness, its frightful human cost, its pathos and loss, and its essential failure to achieve its objectives. Because of that failure it was necessary to fight a Second World War, and if it hadn't been for the subject of Gilbert's biography, England might well have failed to stop Hitler. As prime minister during World War II, Churchill was frequently at odds with his military leaders, and during World War I, as First Lord of the Admiralty and later in other capacities, he also tangled with the military professionals. "Do you think," he asked, writing to his wife from the front in April of 1916, "we should succeed in an offensive, if the Germans cannot do it at Verdun with all their skill and science? Our army is not the same as theirs; and of course their staff is quite intact and taught by successful experiment. Our staff only represents the brain power of our poor peacetime army—with which hardly any really able men would go. We are children at the game compared to them" (238).

Because in important respects Gilbert sees the events of both world wars through Churchill's eyes, this in turn puts him at odds with various military historians, many of them professionally trained soldiers and sailors, who have tended to depict Churchill as an interfering amateur in his dealings with the military, even while readily granting his essential role as leader of his embattled nation during World War II. Among such historians, Gilbert's reputation as a commentator on military affairs is not very high.

A certain amount of snobbery, I am afraid, is at work here, something not exactly unheard of in British social and academic circles. In addition to being a civilian all the way, with his military experience confined to two years of National Service in 1955–1957, Gilbert is a third-generation English Jew of Polish descent. The condescension and resentment with which some English "Establishment" military historians and their disciples have responded to Gilbert's work seems at times to reflect an attitude that he has no right to be writing about such things at all.

In any event, and for whatever reason, Martin Gilbert's history of the First World War is concerned most of all to illustrate the enormous slaughter and wastefulness that were the product of a time in which, to quote Yeats yet again,

> Mere anarchy is loosed upon the world,
> The blood-dimmed tide is loosed, and everywhere
> The ceremony of innocence is drowned . . .
> ("The Second Coming")

Using the skills of the research historian he has combed through wartime letters, diaries, memoirs, accounts of various kinds, seeking to demonstrate the reactions of rank-and-file soldiers to the fighting. Repeatedly he quotes from the poems written by men who are killed in action. The technique throughout is as much that of montage as sequential narrative, with the attention focused upon those who did the fighting, not on those who planned it.

In effect, Gilbert's narrative method replicates the author's attitude toward the war on the Western Front as a thing of largely shapeless horror. A brief summation of the overall military situation at the time of a battle or campaign and a few sentences about what those in command hoped to accomplish are followed by a description of the carnage, with numerous illustrative quotations, and at the close a report on casualties. What comes across is not the military strategy or tactics, but the killing and suffering. As presented, there is a sameness to the successive battlefield ordeals, so that often it becomes difficult to distinguish what went on at the Somme from what took place at Ypres, Loos, Artois, Champagne, Verdun, Vimy Ridge, Passchendaele, Cambrai, the Aisne, etc., other than by casualty figures and proper names—which is precisely Gilbert's point. The tactics employed, the methods of attack and defense, the deployment of the troops involved are largely the same from one battle to the next, just as in almost every instance the results are equally indecisive.

By contrast, a professional military historian such as Cyril Falls goes at the war from a standpoint of the overall strategies employed and how they worked out, with emphasis upon how the military commanders on each side sought to win the war, and how and why they succeeded or failed. Each battle and campaign is depicted as a distinct and recognizable phase in a four-year struggle to defeat the enemy. In *The Great War, 1914–1918,* Falls by no means omits errors and failures, but he sees and depicts the war's military leaders as dedicated professional soldiers confronting an awesome responsibility and doing their best to win the war with the resources available to them. Falls's book provides a great deal more information about the conduct of military and naval operations and the performances of commanders and commanded.

One can understand that as a professional soldier, a participant in the war, and for sixteen years the official British historian of it, Falls would be loath to depict it as a largely botched affair, even though bravely fought. His summation of the ordeal and slaughter of the Somme, for example, is as follows: "Only high hearts, splendid courage, and the enormous endurance of the flower of the nations of the British Empire could have won the results attained. Only wonderful powers of resistance by the Germans could have limited them to what they were" (208).

But what Falls's approach cannot do well is to convey the nature of World War I as what it so agonizingly was for those who fought it: a human disaster, a mass slaughter made only the more dreadful by the knowledge that it accomplished so little. Martin Gilbert's summation for the Somme campaign, by contrast, reads this way: "After four-and-a-half months of struggle, suffering and advance there was no concluding victory, or even coda: one divisional history recorded that two companies which had taken part in the assault on November 18 had disappeared 'entirely, being overwhelmed by machine-gun fire'" (299).

For Gilbert, the dreary fact about the Somme is that despite the horrendous bloodletting of July 1, the attack was renewed the next day, and throughout the subsequent summer and autumn a steady stream of young men continued to be sent over the top to face these rifles, machine guns, and artillery of modern warfare, in a battle of attrition that traded 420,000 British and 204,000 French casualties for 680,000 Germans killed and wounded—in order to take a strip of blasted earth less than ten miles deep at its very broadest, and scarcely twenty-five miles long.

There is something terribly chilling in Cyril Falls's comment about the end of the first day on the Somme, quoted earlier: "Haig must have been bitterly disappointed that night . . . " No doubt the general was indeed disappointed, but, coming after a recounting of the first day's British casualties, the reader may be pardoned for thinking that other things besides Douglas Haig's disappointment might be remarked of the general who had just finished setting a new record, for the English-speaking world in any event, in single-day battle deaths for troops under his command. Whatever may be advanced in criticism of Gilbert's *The First World War: A Complete History*, it cannot be said that he fails to get across to the reader the awesome butcher's bill for the War of 1914–1918. At the same time, if we wish to understand the military strategies and tactics of the Western Front, it is to books such as Cyril Falls's that we must turn.

Military history, if it is to do other than titillate the young and provide chairborne warriors with vicarious combat excitement, must seek to make as much sense as possible of battles and war. Showing the hideousness of it all is not sufficient. At the same time, books about war that neglect to keep the reader continually reminded that what is being described is not a chess game, but that human beings are being maimed and killed by other human beings, can scarcely be said to have made proper sense of the subject, either. To concentrate on the problems of command while neglecting those of the commanded is no way to write about warfare, if the object is to make the experience of war understandable.

It strikes me, in contradiction of the American title of Sir Philip Gibbs's influential memoir of 1920, *Now It Can Be Told*, that even though almost eight decades have gone by since the Armistice, and almost all who took part in the war are dead, a truly definitive account of the First World War has not yet been rendered—or if it has, then I have not read it. The books about the war itself, as distinguished from the circumstances of its advent, continue to fall into two categories, those which effectively describe, interpret, and analyze the strategy and tactics, and those which concentrate on conveying the bloodshed and the horror. Gilbert's book cannot be said to be what its subtitle claims: *The First World War: A Complete History*. It is graphic, it is evocative, but it is not "complete." (To cite an obvious example, no attempt is made to show what that first day on the Somme might have looked like from the German side of No-Man's-Land.) The "complete" history—by which I mean not in its details so much as in its perspective on the war—remains unwritten. We do not yet have an account of the First World War that does justice to the military history while also thoroughly recounting the shock and trauma of trench warfare on the Western Front.

It seems likely that to get such a book, or series of books, we will have to wait for at least as long as it proved necessary to do for a definitive history of the American Civil War—which is to say, until someone approaching the task with literary skill and historical rigor comparable to Shelby Foote's can manage the perspective and insight needed to master the subject. Ninety-three years had elapsed after the surrender of the last Confederate army before the first book of Foote's three-volume *The Civil War: A Narrative* appeared in 1958.

It was not merely happenstance, I think, that the first volume of Shelby Foote's *The Civil War* was published four years after the *Brown v. Board of Education* decision was handed down by the U.S. Supreme Court. The Court's desegregation decision and Foote's Civil War trilogy were equally products of the zeitgeist—to use a term drawn from a time when Germany was famed for its savants and artists rather than for less civilized kinds of activity. The intellectual and emotional climate was finally at a stage at which intellectual judgments could be sustained without diluting the author's sympathy for the human beings caught in the historical trap. There could be sound military history without the suspension of the knowledge of good and evil.

When will that become possible for the War of 1914–1918? Not for a long while, one suspects. In Martin Gilbert's moving book there is a photograph of the battlefield of third Ypres, September 1917. The earth is a torn morass of mud and clods, stretching to the uneven horizon. The half-buried corpse of a soldier is sprawled in the foreground, appearing, in the black-and-white photograph, almost as if it were part of the terrain. Earlier in the book another photograph shows the people of Munich welcoming the coming of war in 1914. Around one of the throng of faces in the crowd is a circle, and an enlarged inset reveals an enthusiastic young Adolf Hitler.

4

High Tide at Jutland

(2001)

It can be argued that the greatest mistake made by the Germany of Kaiser Wilhelm II, apart from giving Austria-Hungary the blank check that turned what might have been a localized dispute into a catastrophic world war, was the decision to build a High Seas Fleet. By creating a naval force that was clearly intended to challenge England's, and no one else's, Imperial Germany ensured that when a European war did come, if Great Britain was involved it would be on the opposing side. Beyond question it was the naval race of the early 1900s that was instrumental in converting British public opinion from being mildly pro- to intensely anti-German, and that brought an end to a century of "splendid isolation" from continental alliances and ententes.

The culminating event of that naval race, the Battle of Jutland, remains one of the most written-about of engagements. Fought between the Grand Fleet of Great Britain and the High Seas Fleet of Imperial Germany in the North Sea off the coast of Denmark on May 31 and June 1, 1916, it was the largest and the last full-fledged naval battle between massed fleets of dreadnoughts. A couple of aircraft did make their appearance, but to no effect. No submarines took part, although the fear that they might was a very real factor.

Strategically Jutland changed nothing, and yet it was one of the decisive battles of naval history. During the eighty-five years since it was fought, numerous books have been devoted entirely to it, and there are many more that deal extensively with it. Only Trafalgar has drawn more attention, though it may be that nowadays Midway is coming close.

The immediate impetus for the German decision to build a blue-water navy was the restless, erratic ambition of Wilhelm II to possess a fighting fleet that would rival that of his grandmother Queen Victoria's. That, however, was possible only because the creation of such a fleet, and for just such a purpose, embodied the intense nationalistic ambitions of the recently unified Reich, and in particular of the flourishing German middle class. Having emerged as the dominant continental power in Europe with the defeat of the French in 1870, the Kaiser's Germany now saw Great Britain as its chief rival. Germany's population was far larger, its industrial production superior, its army much more powerful. Yet there were the British Isles, located geographically athwart Germany's access to the open ocean, a portal that could be slammed shut. The British Empire was the Ruler of the Waves, its colonies and dominions spread over the globe, its merchant marine transporting a major portion of the world's commerce, its Royal Navy twice the size of any other nation's. And the English *knew* it, too; they were accustomed to a position of preeminence.

Not much was needed to encourage German public opinion to begin viewing England as the antagonist. Economic rivalry furthered it, and various incidents abetted it. Still, the ultimate motivation for German militarism was probably much the same as that for the France of Bonaparte and of Louis XIV, and the Spain of Philip II before that: the assertion of supremacy.

The Prussian military tradition, and the dominance of the Junker aristocracy, was of long standing. The navy, however, had scarcely existed before 1870. Its coming into being was an expression of the technological efficiency, the commercial ascendancy, and the growing industrial might of an expanding nation, come lately to empire in an age of rampant imperialism and deficient in colonial possessions.

The justification advanced for creating the High Seas Fleet was security for the German merchant marine and the links with the Reich's recently acquired colonial empire. The navy that the Germans proceeded to build, however, was clearly intended for duty in the North Sea—i.e., against the British. Its major warships were not designed or equipped for lengthy seagoing.

As for England, the long decades following Waterloo had brought prosperity, and with it complacency. Insufficient heed was given to the fact that by the 1880s the economy was in decline, the educational system was increasingly inadequate and in need of revamping, and the English class structure all too stiflingly restrictive. That both Germany and the United States had caught up to and surpassed Great Britain in population and in industrial production seemed scarcely to register.

In 1898 and 1900, the German Reichstag enacted naval bills which together called for a High Seas Fleet of thirty-eight battleships, twenty armored cruisers, and thirty-eight light cruisers, more than double its previous size. The German theory was that such a fleet would be, in Admiral Alfred von Tirpitz's formulation, "so strong that even for the adversary with the greatest sea power a war against it would involve such dangers as to imperil his position in the world" (quoted in Robert Massie, *Dreadnought: Britain, Germany, and the Coming of the Great War* [1991], 181). In other words, the British fleet, although remaining more powerful than Germany's, would dare not risk battle, because even if it won its losses in ships would jeopardize the Royal Navy's continued command of the seas.

The decision to build a fleet to rival England's was opposed by not only German liberals but also some conservatives. As Friedrich von Holstein, a longtime German diplomatic official, warned in 1906, "It is *not* economic rivalry alone that has made England our enemy. . . . What is frightening the English is our accelerated fleet building and the anti-English motivation behind it" (*Holstein Papers: Correspondence, IV: 1897–1909*, 449).

All such caveats were wasted. By 1914 there were more than a million members of a German Navy League dedicated to the proposition that the Reich's rightful place in the world was being blocked by England. Industrialists, academics, chambers of commerce, propagandists of all kinds trumpeted the glories of a German fleet and the inevitability of an eventual showdown with the Royal Navy.

Until Germany began to build a fighting navy, France had been England's assumed rival, but now it became obvious to the British what was going on beyond the North Sea—the more so when, after the abortive Jameson Raid in South Africa, Kaiser Wilhelm II gratuitously expressed public sympathy for the Boers. The stage was set for an all-out naval race.

Thereafter the British outbuilt the Germans. In 1906 the Royal Navy launched the first super-battleship, HMS *Dreadnought*, 17,900 tons displacement, with ten 12-inch guns for its main armament and steam turbine engines capable of 21 knots. Its existence rendered obsolete all other battleships the world over. This was followed by the battlecruiser HMS *Invincible*, a new variety of warship, similar to *Dreadnought* in size and armament but faster and with less protective armor. By the time that war came in 1914 the Royal Navy had twenty dreadnoughts and twelve more under construction, along with nine battlecruisers. Germany responded with thirteen dreadnoughts, seven more being built, and five battlecruisers. The increased cost to the Germans, whose army was the most powerful—and most expensive—in Europe, was enormous. In 1905 the German military budget was 35 percent lower than Britain's; by 1914 it was 40 percent higher.

Once the war began the British Grand Fleet, instead of steaming promptly across the North Sea to do battle, set up a distant blockade, barring the importation of strategic material and foodstuffs for the embattled Reich. German merchant commerce quickly disappeared from the seas. The Kaiser issued orders that the High Seas Fleet was to risk challenging the Royal Navy only when close to its own bases. It could make raids on British channel ports, but must avoid a general action. This meant that its only hope would be to catch a segment of the Grand Fleet and destroy it before the full fleet could interfere.

It was with that goal in mind that during the final days of May 1916, the High Seas Fleet set up what it intended to be a trap to lure a portion of the British fleet to a point at which the German dreadnoughts could get at them. Admiral Reinhard Scheer, commander of the High Seas Fleet, planned a prominently advertised cruiser sweep along the mouth of the Skaggerak, the hundred-mile-wide entrance to the Baltic Sea lying between the southern tip of Norway and the Danish coast. When the British battlecruisers, moving to intercept it, left their bases, German submarines would be waiting offshore for them. Meanwhile the High Seas Fleet would follow its cruisers north, and be ready to pounce upon the British ships that came into the Skaggerak after the German cruisers.

What the German Navy did not realize was that the British were reading its wireless communications. Thus on the morning of May 30, 1916, when elements of the High Seas Fleet were ordered to assemble at the entrance to the Jade River Bay off Wilhelmshaven, the Royal Navy quickly learned of it. By 11:30 that evening, two and one-half hours before the High Seas Fleet set out, the Grand Sea Fleet had departed its anchorages and was headed for a rendezvous fifty miles west of Jutland in the North Sea.

The German U-boat ambush failed, and by the next morning not merely the British battlecruisers but the entire Grand Fleet was steaming steadily eastward, while the High Seas Fleet moved northward up the Danish coast. Each side was unaware that the other had put at sea. The result was the Battle of Jutland.

At the lead of the German fleet was Admiral Franz von Hipper, with five battlecruisers and a screen of light cruisers and destroyers, fifty miles ahead of the main body under Scheer with sixteen dreadnoughts, six slow and poorly armed pre-dreadnoughts, and a variety of armored cruisers, cruisers, and destroyers. The British Grand Fleet, under the command of Admiral Sir John Jellicoe, was in three groups, with twenty-four dreadnoughts and three battlecruisers in the main body, and, not quite seventy miles to the south, six battlecruisers under Admiral David Beatty and four fast dreadnoughts under Admiral Hugh Evan-Thomas. Each capital ship segment was screened by cruisers and destroyers. In all there were 151 British and 100 German vessels.

The British fleet very much outgunned their enemy, with longer-ranged guns throwing a more powerful broadside. Its dreadnoughts and battlecruisers were equipped for director firing, whereby an entire ship's main armament could be aimed and fired as one. But German range-finding optics were superior; German armor-piercing shells were considerably more reliable, and exploded after penetration rather than shattering upon impact at oblique angles; and German ships were more sturdy, of broader beam, with honeycombed bulkhead arrangements that made them less sinkable, and heavier deck armor protecting them against plunging fire.

Winston Churchill, writing in the mid-1920s, made a famous comment about Admiral John Jellicoe, that he "was the only man on either side who could lose the war in an afternoon" (*The World Crisis* 3: 110). A disaster to the Grand Fleet could break the British naval blockade of Europe, cut off the British Army in France from its base of supply, and expose the British Isles themselves to invasion. Jellicoe knew this very well. If he could decisively defeat the German High Seas Fleet, that would be highly desirable, but in Churchill's words, "We were under no compulsion to fight a naval battle except under conditions which made victory morally certain and serious defeat, as far as human vision goes, impossible" (110).

Jellicoe was a systematizer, a man of deliberate ways. Unable to delegate authority, upon assuming command he had acted to develop procedures that would cover every possible eventuality. His Grand Fleet Battle Orders were two hundred pages long. Fearful of encountering mines and torpedoes, he placed severe restraints upon the ability of the Grand Fleet's component divisions to respond to unexpected developments. His aim was centralized control; in striving for that he produced subordinates who preferred to wait for instructions from the flagship before acting.

Jellicoe's plan was for Beatty and his six battlecruisers, with Evan-Thomas's four new dreadnoughts following close by, to head eastward to a point approximately 250 miles distant from their base in the Firth of Forth. If by then no contact had been made with the enemy, Beatty was to turn north by east to join Jellicoe and the oncoming Grand Fleet, with a rendezvous set for 2 p.m. on May 31, 90 miles southwest of the Skaggerak. Meanwhile the German High Seas Fleet was steaming northward up the Jutland coast, with Hipper's battlecruisers no more than 25 miles away from Beatty's scouting force.

It was during Beatty's turn toward Jellicoe that a British light cruiser, sent to investigate a Danish merchant ship, spotted two German destroyers also engaged in doing so. The British cruiser opened fire. The German battlecruiser vanguard swung westward toward the action, while Beatty's battlecruisers reversed course to south-southeastward. Not quite two hours later the two battlecruiser forces were within range of each other, and the battle of Jutland was under way.

The British ships were silhouetted against the western sky, and the initial German firing was more accurate. Beatty's flagship *Lion* was hit hard. Another German salvo struck the older battlecruiser *Indefatigable,* setting off a flash fire that reached its magazine, and the 18,460-ton vessel exploded and sank. Beatty's signal to turn had not been properly relayed to Evan-Thomas's dreadnoughts, which continued northward for ten more minutes before turning to follow. The result was that ten miles separated the two British forces. When after twenty minutes the British dreadnoughts began drawing within range and their 15-inch guns opened fire, their shooting was far better than that of the battlecruisers, and the Germans too began taking severe hits. But another well-aimed German salvo landed squarely on the newer battlecruiser *Queen Mary,* 26,700 tons, with the flash again igniting the magazine and blowing up the warship. It was then that Beatty, from the bridge of *Lion,* made his understandable and oft-cited comment that "There seems to be something wrong with our bloody ships today!" (quoted in Andrew Gordon, *The Rules of the Game: Jutland and British Naval Command* [1996], 120).

At 4:38 p.m. the light cruiser *Southampton* flashed word that the main German fleet had been sighted, whereupon Beatty ordered a 180-degree turn northward, and pursuer and pursued swapped roles. It was now Beatty's turn to try to lead the oncoming Germans toward Jellicoe's battle fleet, thirty-five miles distant and steaming southeastward to join the fight.

At this juncture there occurred one of the most controversial episodes of a battle studded with controversy. Evan-Thomas's dreadnoughts, which were still speeding southward while firing away at Hipper's ships, again failed to turn at once and follow the battlecruisers northward. Apparently the signal to do so was not made operational until three minutes after *Barham,* Evan-Thomas's flagship, passed Beatty and *Lion.* Much post-Jutland dispute centered on whether Evan-Thomas should on his own initiative have proceeded to fall in behind Beatty's battlecruisers, and whether the turn should have been made simultaneously rather than one ship after another.

As the northward chase continued, the rearmost of Evan-Thomas's dreadnoughts took punishment before drawing out of range, while also handing out a great deal of the same to the Germans. The British battlecruisers were angling north-northeast, Beatty and *Lion* in the lead, while Jellicoe and the dreadnoughts of the Grand Fleet were moving southeastward in six columns, preceded by a screen of armored cruisers, and with three battlecruisers under Admiral Horace Hood well up ahead to the southeast.

By six p.m., with three hours of daylight remaining in that northern latitude but visibility difficult because of mist and smoke, the Grand Fleet sighted *Lion,* well to the southwest of where the battlecruisers had been expected. Jellicoe thereupon ordered his dreadnoughts to deploy in line of battle to port, a maneuver that took fifteen to twenty minutes. When done, it not only gave the British the visual advantage of being east of the High Seas Fleet but put the twenty-four dreadnoughts in position to move vertically across the strung-out German battle line, "crossing the T" and allowing them to use the majority of their heavy guns, while greatly restricting the number that Scheer's dreadnoughts could employ.

In the most recent and I think best of all books on Jutland, *The Rules of the Game,* Andrew Gordon points out that one would assume, from the direction in which Beatty had been angling, that Scheer might have suspected that there might be more to what he was doing than an attempt to run away. Yet not until the salvos of heavy shells began falling among the High Seas Fleet did the German commander realize that he, not Beatty, had fallen into a trap.

The visibility now favored the British, who could see the Germans while they themselves were largely hidden by the mist and smoke. To extricate his dreadnoughts Scheer ordered a simultaneous turn westward. He later claimed he had no intention of avoiding battle, but clearly he was bent on withdrawing posthaste. The German ships, in particular the battlecruisers, took heavy punishment; a light cruiser was sunk and the battlecruiser *Lützow* so badly mauled that it went down during the night.

While that was happening, a squadron of obsolescent British armored cruisers quixotically steered between the two fleets; one was destroyed and another later failed to make it back home. Next a momentary break in the mist exposed HMS *Invincible* to Hipper's guns, a well-placed salvo penetrated a gun turret, and for the third time that afternoon a magazine explosion demolished a British battlecruiser.

The well-trained German dreadnoughts executed their tricky 180-degree turn away without flaw and steamed southwestward, while the cruisers and destroyers sent a line of torpedoes streaking toward the Grand Fleet. One torpedo hit the dreadnought *Marlborough;* the others were avoided by a turn away. The High Seas Fleet had moved out of Jellicoe's sight, however, and the British commander received no reports from those who could see what was going on.

At this point, for reasons never fully understood, Scheer executed another 180-degree turn and led the High Seas Fleet right back into trouble. Whatever the explanation for the move, his adversary was given a second chance to wreak havoc with the German High Seas Fleet.

Upon realizing his predicament the German admiral signaled to his already much-mauled battlecruisers to head for the enemy, then ordered a torpedo attack from his destroyer screen, followed by yet another turnaround by his dreadnoughts. Jellicoe's response to the torpedo threat was once again to order the British dreadnoughts to turn away. By the time that they returned to the attack, the peril to the Germans was considerably reduced.

Once darkness intervened, the prospects for a slugging match between dreadnoughts were gone. Jellicoe had no intention whatever of fighting a night action. Too much would be left to chance confrontations; without a destroyer-cruiser screen it would be too easy for his capital ships to blunder into the path of torpedoes. The Germans were better equipped for night fighting and better rehearsed at it.

Scheer and the High Seas Fleet steered east-southeast, aiming for the Jutland coast below the Horn Reef, from where he could take shelter behind minefields for the journey back to Wilhelmshaven. The British admiral, uncertain which escape route the Germans would choose, headed south, with his battlecruisers well to the west of his dreadnoughts. There was ample evidence to deduce the High Seas Fleet's route, but almost nothing was reported to Jellicoe. In actuality the rival fleets were on converging courses, with the British in the lead, and at some point close to midnight the German dreadnoughts crossed through and astern of the British van. During the night an older British armored cruiser and a German pre-dreadnought battleship were lost, together with a German light cruiser and destroyers on both sides. When dawn came shortly after 3 a.m., a heavy mist lay over the coastal waters, and by the time Jellicoe could have gone into action Scheer's fleet was safe from further attack. The Battle of Jutland, or the Skaggerak as the Germans termed it, was over.

The argument about it had only begun. Upon arrival at Wilhelmshaven the Germans proclaimed victory. Kaiser Wilhelm II announced that "the spell of Trafalgar had been broken" and bestowed decorations and promotions (Gordon, 498). The German press exulted. In terms of ships, tonnage, and men lost, there could be no question that the count favored the High Seas Fleet. The British had lost three battlecruisers, three older armored cruisers, and eight destroyers, totaling 115,025 tons, as against a single battlecruiser, a predreadnought, four light cruisers, and five destroyers, in all 61,180 tons. The cost in lives was 6,094 for the Grand Fleet, 2,551 for the High Seas Fleet. In damage sustained, however, the surviving German ships had been hit hard; as a fighting force the High Seas Fleet was out of commission for some weeks to come, while within twenty-four hours after returning to base Jellicoe's fleet was ready for action.

For the British Grand Fleet, Jutland was scarcely a well-fought battle. "There is something wrong with our ships," David Beatty repeated aboard *Lion* the afternoon following, and he added, "and something wrong with our system" (Gordon, 495-96). Jellicoe himself was deeply depressed. Yet what mattered most was that nothing had been changed strategically. The battle fleets had met, and the High Seas Fleet had fled, with the Grand Fleet in pursuit. Scheer had not isolated and trapped a segment of the Grand Fleet and equalized the odds for a future decisive battle. On the contrary, the German admiral was now convinced that there was no way that the High Seas Fleet could alter the course of the war, and he informed the Kaiser that "a victorious end to the war within a reasonable time can only be achieved through the defeat of British economic life—that is, by using the U-boats against British trade" (quoted in Gordon, 415). In other words, Scheer advocated the resumption of unrestricted submarine warfare, which would probably have the effect of bringing the United States into the war on the Allies' side. The German emperor reluctantly consented. The results of this decision would prove to be almost incalculable.

As for Great Britain, what Jutland did show, and all too clearly, was that there were serious deficiencies in His Majesty's Fleet and its mode of operation. No less than three British battlecruisers had exploded and gone down, with tremendous loss of life, upon being struck by salvos that triggered flash fires and reached the magazines. The big-gun ammunition was unreliable, and its lyddite charges in-efficient; investigation revealed lax manufacturing standards and slipshod inspection procedures. Signaling procedures were haphaz-ard; again and again orders given by flag were not repeated with searchlights, and not passed on from ship to ship.

Throughout the battle there was a failure to keep Jellicoe informed of what was happening. Ship captains repeatedly assumed that the Grand Fleet commander could see whatever they saw, which was by no means always true. When on several occasions during the night the shapes of what could only have been crippled German battle-cruisers were observed, they were not fired on for fear that they might be British, nor was Jellicoe notified of their presence.

In the controversy over Jutland that ensued, what has been most at issue has not been whether the British or German fleet can be said to have "won" the battle, but the Grand Fleet's inability to win a Trafalgar-like victory, and whether it might have been expected to do so. On the one side is the argument that John Jellicoe's responsi-bility was not to fight and win a major battle. His task was essentially defensive and in this he succeeded. As Richard Hough declared in *The Great War at Sea, 1914–1918* (1983), "Germany could play with figures for as long as she wished, but British control of the world's sea lanes was unimpaired, the blockade of the enemy as tight as ever" (297).

On the other hand, it can be argued that in developing a two-hundred-page set of battle orders and expecting total conformity to them, Jellicoe had trained a set of subordinates to expect that all their decisions would be made for them. In Hough's words, "Jellicoe did not encourage consultation and did not care for any questioning of what he had laid down" (272). At Jutland the Grand Fleet division commanders and most flotilla captains had only done what they had been encouraged to do: wait for instructions, interpret them conser-vatively, and play it safe.

Thus when Evan-Thomas with the new dreadnoughts failed to follow Beatty's turn to the south as the battle opened, he was wait-ing for an order to do it. When two hours later he continued to steer in the direction of the oncoming High Seas Fleet even after his flag-ship passed Beatty's battlecruisers headed northward, he was again waiting for an order. Others of Jellicoe's captains showed a similar absence of enterprise.

As for Jellicoe himself, the tactical decisions for which he was most often criticized in after years were establishing his line of battle to port rather than starboard—i.e., away from the action—when his dreadnoughts prepared to enter the fighting, and then twice turning away from instead of toward his opponent to avoid the torpedoes fired by Scheer's destroyers.

It is generally agreed nowadays that his choice of a swing to port to form his dreadnoughts into a fighting line was justified, and indeed it placed him in an excellent position to pulverize the oncoming German fleet. His second turn-away from the torpedoes in particular, however, and how it was done, was dubious. Andrew Gordon, describing Jellicoe's response, declares that "At this juncture Edward Hawke or Adam Duncan (and, perhaps, David Farragut) would have turned the Grand Fleet, by divisions, towards the enemy" (464; for reasons to be remarked later, the "perhaps," set off by commas, is delicious). In Richard Hough's summation, "This was the moment when to turn from the defensive to the offensive posed none of the risks [from submarines and mines] Jellicoe had always feared. . . . This failure to follow up the enemy, whose tactical position was a shambles, and destroy almost certainly Hipper's battlecruisers, and very likely half a dozen of Scheer's most valuable dreadnoughts, is a serious and valid criticism of Jellicoe's leadership" (287).

David Beatty thought and later said as much, and it is the supporters of Beatty who argued that there should have been a devastating British victory at Jutland. To be sure, Beatty has by no means been without his own critics. He retained a signals officer who had on a previous occasion demonstrated his incompetence. Before he went in pursuit of the German battlecruisers after the first sighting, he failed to see that his force was properly closed on him. He did not keep Jellicoe properly informed after he had turned back northward; not until the following day, when the battle was over, did Jellicoe learn of the loss of *Indefatigable* and *Queen Mary*.

As a man Beatty was self-serving, deceitful, in Gordon's term something of a bounder. Yet his aggressive fighting talents were what had twice provided Jellicoe with the opportunity to devastate the German fleet. He went after the enemy. He understood the importance of encouraging initiative and responsibility. He was willing to take losses in order to ensure triumph. When later he succeeded to command of the Grand Fleet he vastly simplified the basic principles for action in battle, with far more emphasis on the need for his captains to act for themselves when opportunity presented. It was Beatty's example, and not Jellicoe's, that Philip Vian followed a quarter-century later when without orders he broke away from escorting a convoy and sped to join the attack on the *Bismarck*, and that Andrew Cunningham employed against the Italians at Cape Matapan.

Much of what has been written about Jutland in the years immediately following World War I was based upon the accounts published by various participants. Later books, such as Arthur Marder's multivolume *From the Dreadnought to Scapa Flow* (1966), have sought to interpret the documentary evidence with less prejudgment. I want to note three recent studies of Jutland by British historians: V. E. Tarrant's *Jutland: The German Perspective: A New View of the Great Battle, 31 May 1916* (1995), N. J. M. Campbell's *Jutland: An Analysis of the Fighting* (1986), and Andrew Gordon's *The Rules of the Game*. To different degrees all three are useful to anyone wishing to understand the battle, and the value of Gordon's book goes considerably farther than that.

Tarrant chronicles the proceedings of May 31–June 1 as they appeared to the Germans at the time and later, quoting extensively from the official German history published in 1925, the memoirs of Tirpitz and Scheer, and other German accounts. While his book remains even so essentially a British view of Jutland, with the German reports used to provide not so much an alternative vantage point for the narrative as an additional dimension, it enables the reader to get a sense of the battle as involving opposing strategies and tactics. Not the least interesting feature of the book is a summary of the more important German wireless messages and signals in sequence.

Campbell's *Jutland: An Analysis of the Fighting* is not for the casual reader. It offers a meticulous breakdown of what was going on. We are told which ships opened fire on which ships, at what ranges, the courses and speeds made, the signals sent and received, the decisions made and the orders given by the commanders. There is a report, ship by capital ship, on the casualties, the damage each ship suffered, where it occurred, and the probable source of the projectiles, together with diagrams and cross-sections showing the path of the projectiles and the extent of their impact. Campbell was able to get access not only to the British but also to the German post-battle damage analyses. The result includes some correctives to assumptions made in earlier accounts.

He develops a point also made by Arthur Marder in *From the Dreadnought to Scapa Flow,* that in the destruction of the three British battlecruisers the most important factor was that the British projectile charges were kept in silk bags, while those of the High Seas Fleet were in brass cases, which when an enemy shell penetrated the turret had the effect of delaying their ignition, causing them to burn relatively slowly. Thus "no dangerous pressure rise occurred from a number of charges igniting at nearly the same instant, as occurred with British charges" (378). Had British propellant charges been used by the German ships, Campbell declares after examining the evidence, the dreadnought *König* and the battlecruisers *Derfflinger,* probably *Seydlitz,* and possibly *von der Tann* would have suffered the same fate as the British battlecruisers. Campbell doesn't take sides in the Jellicoe-Beatty dispute; it is the ships themselves, not how they were employed, that interest him.

Which brings us to Andrew Gordon's *The Rules of the Game,* a book that, far from being principally for specialists, seems to me to be little short of a major work of military and naval history. *The Rules of the Game* handles its subject so masterfully, and so imaginatively, that one wonders how a better book on the particular topic could ever be written.

Gordon divides his book into five parts—all 690 pages of it, about 230,000 words together with maps, charts, diagrams, plus 40 photographs and a few line drawings. Part I, "Background to Battle," sends the Grand Fleet eastward on what was generally assumed to be yet another useless expedition. Part II, "Chasing Hipper and Eluding Scheer," chronicles the chase southeast, the sighting of the High Seas Fleet, and the run north toward the oncoming Grand Fleet. David Beatty's negligence in keeping the four dreadnoughts closed on his battlecruisers and the inability of his hapless signals officer are fully aired, but it is Hugh Evan-Thomas's unwillingness to think for himself that Gordon sees as the index to what went wrong with the Royal Navy at Jutland.

Why, Gordon asks, did it happen? "Common sense says that Britain's finest battle-squadron should not have found itself, in effect, 'not under command' at this critical juncture, and that, when Beatty passed on his opposite course, an admiral worthy of 120,000 tons of capital ships should have maneuvered them of his own accord." The ultimate explanation, Gordon proposes, was cultural: "the coincidence of mass-production and the social religion of deference" (150). To show how this came to be, he leaves the battle of Jutland to embark on an engrossing 250-page excursion into what he describes as "the long calm lee of Trafalgar."

The technological advances of the nineteenth century, steam power, iron ships, and long-range gunnery, would have produced in any case a need for readjustment, experiment, and revamping of long-established ways of doing things. For the peacetime Royal Navy, however, there were special problems, having to do with the culture, attitudes, and expectations of Victorian England. Naval command was a profession for gentlemen only, and the educational system for upper-class English youths was narrowly classical, with a bias against science and technology. Moreover, embedded in the British class system was the habit of deference to one's superiors. Persons entering the Royal Navy were "subjected to a cultural climate more unremittingly authoritarian than at any other time in British history, for the Victorians sought to structure and codify as many fields of behavior as possible in order to regulate their world, disarm the unpredictable and perpetuate the *status quo*" (179).

To this is added the inevitable tendency of peacetime navies and armies to be the natural habitat of "authoritarian" personalities who do everything by the book, are meticulous about details, attempt to systematize all their activities, and are suspicious of any signs of initiative. Another response to technology in the nineteenth century was an intense revival of the medieval cult of chivalry, "Playing the Game" by the rules, doing only what is "cricket"—"Chivalry was uncerebral, extrovert and physically healthy . . . In Victorian England its most pernicious effect was the confusion of warfare with ritualized team games" (181).

The reply of the Victorian Navy to the unprecedented demands of adjusting the traditional methods of naval warfare to steam-powered ships that could fire on each other from miles off was to attempt to regulate fleet tactics through detailed rules and extensive direction via flag signals. The result was Philip Colomb's *Manual of Fleet Evolutions* (1874), which offered three hundred pages of geometrically precise maneuvers. The flag combinations necessary to accomplish these numbered in the tens of thousands, and a five-hundred-page *Signal Book* was issued to all ships. Hence the title, intended ironically, of Gordon's book.*

There were some who were disturbed by such developments, and who feared that the Royal Navy was in danger of forgetting that its primary mission was to fight. By the early 1890s the advocates of simplification and decentralization were putting their hopes on Vice Admiral Sir George Tryon, a bluff, autocratic old sea dog, no worshipper of authority, who was succeeding to the command of the elite British Mediterranean Fleet. Tryon wanted to break the hold of traditionalism over the Navy, which he thought was throttling initiative, and he believed that the key to doing so was to end the dominance of signaling.

On June 22, 1892, the Mediterranean fleet was maneuvering in parallel columns, with Tryon aboard the battleship *Victoria* at the head of one, and Rear Admiral Albert Markham on *Camperdown* leading the other. Tryon signaled—with flags—for the columns to make 180-degree inward turns in succession, the flagship turning to port and *Camperdown* to starboard, and each subsequent warship following suit. Officers on *Victoria*'s bridge realized that the columns were too close together for the maneuver, but Tryon insisted. As everyone watched to see what would happen, *Victoria* and *Camperdown* turned onto an obvious collision course, *Camperdown*'s bow knifed into the starboard bow of *Victoria*, and within four minutes *Victoria* turned keel up and sank. Some 358 officers and sailors, more than half the flagship's crew, were drowned, among them Sir George

---

*One is reminded of the response of Stonewall Jackson, not an aristocrat, when his men forbore to fire at a Union officer engaged in bravely exposing himself to Confederate gunfire in order to rally his troops. Jackson ordered them to shoot him down; "I do not wish them to be brave."

Tryon. Commander John Jellicoe, ill and confined to his berth, managed to get to the deck and swim away.

No one knew what had gone wrong with Tryon. (The incident was parodied in Alec Guinness's movie *Kind Hearts and Coronets*.) At the subsequent court-martial his flag-captain was acquitted of dereliction of duty, and neither Admiral Markham nor *Camperdown*'s flag-captain was blamed. Thus three high-ranking Royal Navy officers, any one of who by declining to follow an order that was obviously disastrously wrong-headed could have averted the collision, went uncensured and unpunished—for "the best interests of the service," the claim was made.

The implication, so far as the encouragement of intelligent dissent and the exercise of individual judgment in the British Navy were concerned, was all too clear. Andrew Gordon describes the difficulties of reform during the two succeeding decades, in the face of the complex, entwined allegiances of the upholders of the status quo. He also chronicles the pervasive role of the British royalty in advancing the careers of certain favorites, notably Hugh Evan-Thomas. When war came, the stage was set for what happened off the Jutland coast.

The Rules of the Game then resumes the analysis of the battle and the concluding night action in which the German High Seas Fleet made it back to safety. The unwillingness of Evan-Thomas and various of Jellicoe's squadron commanders to act on their own initiative, the automatic assumption by almost everyone that the commander on the flagship must already be aware of what they were seeing, the reluctance to break wireless silence at night when important developments occurred, the general disinclination to act and eagerness to defer to authority—all these are seen as the inevitable outcome of "the structured 'rationalist' certainties of the late Victorian Mediterranean Fleet . . ." (576). By the prescriptive, centralizing premises on which his elaborate battle orders were based, Jellicoe had acted correctly—but they were the premises of the peacetime Victorian era, not Horatio Nelson's.

Gordon describes the post-Jutland controversy between the supporters of Jellicoe and those of Beatty, which by the time the war ended was in full swing. Beatty's role in the extended dispute is shown as underhanded and unattractive.

This extraordinarily interesting narrative concludes with a chapter entitled "Perspectives," in which the author formulates twenty-eight "syndrones" which, he says, are likely to happen in the peacetime Royal Navy. Most of them are truisms such as *"The key to efficiency lies in the correct balance between organization and method"* (598). This to my mind is the least convincing portion of *The Rules of the Game*. If included at all, the chapter should have been treated as an appendix, not the culmination of the book. The historical insights in Gordon's book are too profound, and in terms of military and naval performance the implications too far-reaching and inferential, to be ticked off in reductive fashion, as if they were little more than a set of cautionary aphorisms.

Yet the very passion with which Gordon goes about proclaiming his set of cautions is emblematic of what makes *The Rules of the Game* so notable a book. The author is deeply and emotionally involved with his subject, even while sufficiently objective not to take sides. His involvement is what leads him, for example, to argue at prodigious length with certain of N. J. M. Campbell's findings. One also gets the sense, too, that Gordon's reluctance to acknowledge the extent to which Arthur Marder's work anticipates his own involves more than disagreement about particular points. What Gordon seems to object to about Marder is his temerity in venturing to write about the Royal Navy at all; it appears to annoy him.

Not only Andrew Gordon's ardor, but N. J. M. Campbell's meticulous computation, and the avidity with which so many British writers have refought Jutland over the years, are an interesting phenomenon. Certainly warfare at sea makes for stirring reading; unlike land warfare it often has a starkness and an absence of contingency about it. And understandably there is a fascination about the last and greatest battle of the dreadnought era. Even so, there seems a kind of obsession about refighting Jutland that suggests the presence of something over and beyond its place in naval history. It bears, in fact, a distinct resemblance to the way that Southern historians have written about the Battle of Gettysburg.

Gettysburg was the High Tide of the Southern Confederacy, and it has been refought on paper ever since, first by the veterans themselves, then by the historians. Over the decades the terms of disputation have become more subtle and the historical involvement more disciplined by methodological rigor. Yet the fervor remains. One-hundred-thirty-eight years and two world wars have not yet extinguished it. The events, the details, the personalities of the leading generals, the ramifications of the failure to win the battle, have been reexamined again and again.

Surely this has to do with the way in which Gettysburg symbolizes the South's failure to win the war and establish its independence. The diminution of the sectional issues that led to secession and that made separate nationhood appear desirable has brought less partisan, more objective history, with less searching about for scapegoats. Yet that history is still far from being cold-bloodedly and dispassionately chronicled. *What went wrong with our army?* This is the implied question.

Much the same kind of impulse would appear to lie behind the continuing hold of Jutland on the British imagination. The memory of Jutland is of an opportunity lost. As such it symbolizes the inability of an island nation to sustain a hundred years of Ruling the Waves. *How could it have happened?* There is a poignancy to it that goes quite beyond any historical determinism. It is not economic logic that is involved, but Heart's Desire.

This, I think, helps to account for the considerable falling off of Andrew Gordon's concluding chapter. Its approach is incongruous with what the book is and is not about. For *The Rules of the Game* is *not* a work of military and naval instruction, in the style of Mahan, Liddell Hart, Fuller et al., in which history is shaped and adapted for teaching purposes. It is history for history's sake, written because the event being described carries so much significance for the author.

The emotional dimension also goes far to explain the occasional snide remarks about Britain's American ally, of which the begrudging reference to David Glasgow Farragut is only one, that crop up here and there, however arbitrarily, in Gordon's book (and indeed much military and naval history written by Britons). The American Navy may not have been involved at Jutland, but symbolically the United States did "win" the battle, in that after World War I it would inherit the role that Victorian and Edwardian England had previously played in the world. Thus the resentment of True British Tars.

Spliced-on "Perspectives" to the contrary notwithstanding, this latest installment in the Jutland dispute is a masterful work. In thoroughness, in imaginative concept, in depth of perception it dwarfs its predecessors. So much so that if military and naval analysis were all that were involved in the choice of subject, as if Jutland were of no more emotional importance than, say, Actium or Oresund, one could even declare that the long-standing Jutland controversy has now been resolved, and no further books about it are in order. Emotionally and historically, however, much more is at stake, which is why the argumentation is likely to continue.

5

Western Front

The Americans Enter the War

(2000)

We may not like the thought of war, but we certainly can't ignore it, and least of all in our own time, having only just concluded a century characterized by the two most murderous wars in human history. World War II has until recently received by far the more attention from military historians. Yet the events of 1939–1945 were nothing less than a continuation of those of 1914–1918, and now that the surviving veterans of the first war have departed the scene and all those remaining of the second have traveled decisively beyond the biblically assigned three-score-and-ten, historians have been training their sights upon the military history of World War I. In particular the Western Front has been a prime target.

The conflict that turned our twentieth century into the most brutalized in recorded history is still often referred to as the Great War, even though the resumption that began formally in 1939 and ended in 1945 was far more lethal—fifty million killed as against a mere ten million (some say twelve), more nearly worldwide in scope, and more decisive in its outcome. Whatever it is called, World War I was largely fought by armed men against other armed men, and as John Keegan notes in *The First World War* (1999), it "saw no systematic displacement of populations, no deliberate starvation, no expropriation, little massacre or atrocity. It was, despite the effort by state propaganda machines to prove otherwise, and the cruelties of the battlefield apart, a curiously civilized war" (8).

It exercises its hold upon historians in part because, with all its cataclysmic consequences, its outbreak was so manifestly avoidable. The succession of events from the assassination of the Austrian Archduke by Serbian nationalists on June 28, 1914, up to the German assault upon Liege on August 4 that put the hostilities beyond rescission might at almost any stage have been interrupted and arrested. None of the governments of the major belligerents, not even the saber-rattling Reich of Kaiser Wilhelm II, desired full-fledged war to happen. There was no Adolf Hitler at the helm of any of the European powers, who had gained dictatorial office on a promise to avenge his country's earlier defeat.

What happened in 1939 does not lead historians to search for the origins or to argue about who the principal perpetrators were. By contrast, books still appear with some regularity attempting to apportion the blame for the debacle of 1914. I read one a few years ago that managed principally to blame the French, which required considerable ingenuity even for a card-carrying revisionist.

There is a popular image of the First World War consisting of multi-thousands of young Britons, Frenchmen, and Germans being marched out into No-Man's-Land on the Western Front to be mowed down by machine-gun fire or blasted into oblivion by artillery, year after year for four years. The role of the United States in the fighting was to send an army over toward the end—"The Yanks are coming"—thereby tipping the balance in favor of the Allied side, and causing the Germans to run out of manpower and to ask for an armistice.

The fighting on the Western Front did indeed resemble a slaughterhouse; the generals in command did seem able to find nothing better to do than to try to wear down each others' armies by sheer attrition. As for the United States, once the Americans had shown they could hit hard and keep hitting, beyond doubt the advent of the American Expeditionary Force in France during the spring and summer of 1918 did cause the Germans to abandon all hope of victory and to sue for terms.

On the other hand, militarily there was in fact decided innovation in the methods of attack on the Western Front during the last couple of years. The British developed tank warfare, air power became a considerable factor in the fighting, and the Germans evolved tactics for breaking through the four-year stalemate of trench warfare. As for the capabilities of the various high commands, while nobody would have given any of the leading generals on either side high marks for innovative tactical skill, the basic problem was not so much their shortcomings in imagination as that the development of the defensive weaponry of modern industrial war had reached a stage well in advance of the ability to direct and sustain offensive war against it.

John Keegan sees not only the protracted slaughter but the actual coming of war itself as essentially a failure in the development of communications. The generals were unable to exercise any real control over the conduct of their armies once their planned offensives commenced, and thus left them vulnerable to the enormous destructiveness of modern artillery and machine-gun weaponry, which without considerably more innovation in the tactics of the attacking force than was customary in the trench warfare of the Western Front always favored the defenders.

For their part, the diplomatists of the negotiating governments could not keep pace with the greatly enhanced rapidity with which twentieth-century European armies could be mobilized and set to fighting each other. "Information arrived fitfully, sometimes much, sometimes little, but it was always incomplete," Keegan writes. "There was no way of correlating and displaying it, as there is in modern crisis management centres. . . ." (59) There was almost a total absence of means for negotiating delays in the seemingly remorseless sequence of events. No United Nations, no councils or forums were available for extending and broadening discussions and circulating proposals and responses. The fate of peace was in the hands of isolated, divergent individuals, some of whom were reckless, others all too casual in their responses to the growing crisis.

A general conflict might have still been avoided following Austria's declaration of war against Serbia, had not Helmuth von Moltke the younger vastly exceeded the authority that as chief of staff he possessed "even," as Keegan adds, "in militaristic Germany." In defiance of his own government's efforts to persuade Austria to localize the conflict, that gentleman telegraphed the Austrian chief of staff, urging him to "stand firm against Russian mobilization" with a mobilization of his own, and promising that Germany would do the same (64). It was the second such blank check issued to Austria by Germany; earlier the Kaiser himself had assured Emperor Franz Joseph that he could "rely on Germany's full support" (53)—and then immediately departed on a vacation cruise. Without German backing, Austria was in no shape to risk a major war; with that backing, Austria went recklessly ahead.

If there was a root cause for World War I, Keegan suggests, it was "the dissatisfaction of the German-speaking peoples with their standing among other nations" (9). This seems plausible to me. Tsarist Russia, to be sure, bears some of the responsibility, both for having encouraged Serbia and for its momentous decision to begin mobilization. France, for its part, by pledging its support if Russia were attacked by Germany, undoubtedly bolstered Russia's willingness to back Serbia at the risk of war. But it was Germany, more so than any other major European power, which had helped create the atmosphere of advanced national tensions in which war was likely to break out, and then when the crisis came had impetuously assured the Austrian government of its full support, no matter what.

In contrast to the trouble-plagued Hapsburg Empire, the Germany of the early 1900s was flexing its muscles after its successful unification, engineered by Otto von Bismarck in a manner that made it largely free of democratic controls over the military. Wilhelmine Germany throbbed with nervous energy; it was jealous of England's and France's colonial possessions, and as the leading industrial nation in Europe desired what it considered its right to increased status and influence. Power was concentrated in the person of the Kaiser; he had no obligation to keep the various branches and ministries of his government informed, and his military high command, not the elected civilian government, was calling the shots.

Wilhelm II's erratic drum-beating, posturing, and meddling, the creation of a powerful High Seas fleet that could only be meant to challenge England, the repeated gratuitous intrusions into potential trouble spots in Samoa, the Philippines, South Africa, Venezuela, Morocco, China, and elsewhere—these and other provocative actions cannot be explained by economic factors alone. "Deutschland, Deutschland Uber Alles, / Uber Alles In Der Welt," as the *Kaisershymne* so aptly put it.

Germany's blueprint for action when war came, the Schlieffen Plan, called for Belgium's borders to be violated so that France could be attacked from the north and knocked out of the war in time to transfer the Reich's armies eastward via the German railway network and smash the ponderous Russian advance. When at the last moment its Emperor sought to halt the attack on France across Belgian soil, he was told by his chief of staff that the long-readied war plan could not be interrupted, and, in Keegan's words, he "panicked and let a piece of paper determine events" (47).

The "piece of paper," the long-nurtured Schlieffen Plan, failed. Although hit hard, France was not knocked out of the war, and there was stalemate on the Western Front, with the opposing armies installed in a system of trenches stretching from the English Channel to the border of Switzerland. Thereafter offensive after offensive was mounted, to be repelled each time with lavish expenditure of human lives. In 1915, 1916, and 1917, as casualty figures reached the millions, the generals could think only to send new waves of troops Over the Top.

Offensives were preceded by days of shelling by massed artillery. Aerial observation made it possible to direct artillery with greater effectiveness. New tools of destruction such as poison gas provided additional methods of killing. Rail transportation enabled reserves to be moved swiftly in position to contain and then erase the gains made from breakthroughs. The generals of the First World War, Keegan says, were "trapped within the iron fetters of a technology all too adequate for mass destruction of life but quite inadequate to restore to them the flexibilities of control that would have kept destruction of life within bearable limits" (316).

Lacking radio or wireless telegraphy and with field telephone and telegraph lines soon blasted into shreds, those in command were unable to give direction to what was going on. The farther the advance, the greater the loss of coordination. Attacking infantry quickly lost touch with the supporting artillery. Breakthroughs could not be exploited, accurate barrages called in, or reinforcements directed where needed. Once reaching their immediate objectives, the attackers were cut off from support and became vulnerable to counterattack. The tactical advantage passed over to the defenders, while a murderous bombardment made withdrawal possible only at terrible cost.

The enlarged scale of the fighting forced the generals of the Western Front to locate themselves far behind the lines, where once an offensive began they could only wait, sometimes for entire days and longer, to discover what was happening. After the first day of the Somme offensive in 1916, to cite one example, when sixty thousand British soldiers were killed or wounded, General Douglas Haig had no idea of the enormity of his losses, and was prepared to resume the attack the next day. The Germans, he announced, had "undoubtedly been severely shaken," when in fact their losses were no more than a tenth of the British army's (Keegan, 295).

In 1917, over the objections of Prime Minister David Lloyd George who saw little prospect that yet another offensive could dislodge the well-entrenched Germans, the British commander insisted on pouring more hundreds of thousands of men into the morass of Third Ypres. "On the Somme," Keegan writes, Haig "had sent the flower of British youth to death or mutilation; at Passchendaele he had tipped the survivors into the slough of despond" (369). It was the civilian government's duty, he believed, to provide him with replacements as needed to mount additional offensives, without asking any questions. No diversions were to be made from the needs of the Western Front, no allocation of troops and resources elsewhere was acceptable. Mystically optimistic, he was always convinced that the next attack, the next penetration would produce the long-awaited breakthrough.

Particularly following the bloodbath that the year 1916 had proved to be on all sides, there were sporadic attempts to get the nations involved to come to their senses and accept the fact that nothing that might be won could compensate for the additional loss in lives and property that further fighting must surely involve. But no serious effort was made to negotiate; the terms that each warring power let it be known would be its minimum requirements precluded any cessation. When in January of 1918 the American president, Woodrow Wilson, proposed as a basis for peace his Fourteen Points, which called for evacuation of all enemy territory occupied by the opposing armies, the return of Alsace and Lorraine to France, and essentially a peace without victory, neither side was interested. God Himself only needed ten points, the French premier Georges Clemenceau declared.

Indeed, as late as early July of 1918 the Kaiser, his government, and the German high command were in agreement that "to complement the acquisition of territories in the east, the annexation of Luxembourg and the French iron and coal fields in Lorraine were necessary and minimum terms for concluding the war in the west" (408). By then the Ludendorff offensive that was designed to end the war before the Americans could make an impact was all but spent, and no more German infantry replacements were available. Twenty-five American divisions in various stages of readiness were in France and 250,000 more troops were arriving each month, the British naval blockade was tightening, there were food shortages at home, and the police were reporting civilian unrest in Berlin.

So the killing and maiming continued in a four-year war that, in Keegan's words, "damaged civilization, the rational and liberal civilization of the European enlightenment, permanently for the worse and, through the damage done, world civilization also" (8). The totalitarianism that arose in its wake was, as Keegan says, "the political continuation of war by other means" (8), and when after two decades of sporadic violence the full-fledged fighting was renewed in 1939, it was "five times more destructive of human life" than the First World War and "incalculably more costly in material terms . . ." (3)

What I find impressive about Keegan's book is that he has been able to write a military history of World War I that—with, however, one striking exception—offers both a coherent account of the progress of the military campaigns and a continuing depiction of the human cost paid by the men in the contending armies. Previous one-volume histories have in general managed either one or the other, but not both. It is a difficult thing to do, particularly on the Western Front, because of the appalling discrepancy between the intentions of the generals who planned the successive offensives and the inability of the attacking forces to attain their objectives in the face of the terrible killing power of early twentieth-century weaponry. I do think that Keegan has generally been able to handle the warfare without shortchanging its awesome cost.

While emphasizing the Western Front, as is proper, Keegan offers a coherent, well-ordered account of the war on the Eastern Front, ending in the collapse of the Russian armies and the Bolshevik revolution. Considerable attention is also given to the Turkish army's role in the war. The Allies consistently underestimated the capabilities of the Turkish soldiers, who if given capable leadership were formidable fighting men, as demonstrated in the Gallipoli campaign of 1915–1916 when under the German General Liman von Sanders's direction the thirty-four-year-old Mustapha Kemal was able to block a poorly managed Allied drive to capture Constantinople, open the Bosporus, and deliver much-needed help to the faltering Russian war effort.

Up to and including the Ludendorff offensive of March-June 1918, which broke through the Allied position and threatened for a time to imperil the Allies' ability to hold the line on the Western Front, John Keegan's history of World War I is highly satisfactory. Yet at that point, unexpectedly and unaccountably, everything changes, and thereafter he provides only the most sketchy summary of what happened, as if the Allied-American counteroffensive that forced the Germans to seek an armistice were little more than a mopping-up operation.

Having, for example, described the first important tank battle at Cambrai in late 1917, he then shows little interest in the remarkable further development of tank warfare by the British and French, even though at several key junctures in the 1918 fighting—Hamel, Amiens, the Marne—the use of massed tank formations played a notable role in the Allied attack. For a book which earlier had rightly placed great emphasis upon the role of technology in making war on the Western Front what it so destructively was, this failure to follow a very important development in that technology through to its most effective use during the summer of 1918 is surprising.*

Something else, more important even than the tanks, is largely ignored: the role of the American Expeditionary Force in defeating Germany. The impact of the Americans upon German morale, Keegan declares, was such that it was "indeed immaterial whether the doughboys fought well or not. Though the professional opinion of

---

*For an excellent presentation of this topic see Hubert C. Johnson, *Breakthrough: Tactics, Technology, and the Search for Victory on the Western Front in World War I* (1994).

veteran French and British officers that they were enthusiastic rather than efficient was correct, the critical issue was the effect of their arrival on the enemy. It was deeply depressing" (411). Having said that, he seems to have decided that what happened at St. Mihiel and in the Meuse-Argonne campaign was therefore irrelevant, for he does not so much as mention those operations.

Granted that Keegan's book was written for initial publication in England, not in the United States, the failure to describe what was involved in the advent of the American Army is even so an odd omission. That the author likewise declined to describe the successful British and French assault upon the Hindenburg Line is not a satisfactory explanation. The Americans were a crucial addition to the Western Front, and the failure to chronicle their painful introduction to modern warfare constitutes a distinct and arbitrary shortcoming in what is otherwise a notable work of interpretative military history.

There is no more than a sentence on the enormous pressure exerted on the AEF and General John J. Pershing by both the British and French to funnel American troops into the depleted ranks of their own regiments and divisions as replacements, and Pershing's determination to field a separate American army. A description of the role of the Americans in helping to stop the Ludendorff offensive at the Marne is given, and as far as the AEF is concerned, that is it. At no point does the performance of the Americans as a separate army come into Keegan's narrative.

This means, among other things, that there is no discussion whatever as to whether Pershing, in agreeing to uproot his inexperienced army from the St. Mihiel salient as demanded by Marshal Ferdinand Foch and transfer it lock, stock, and barrel into perhaps the toughest, most defensible terrain on the entire Western Front, was not being manipulated for other than purely military reasons. Precisely that charge has been made by others. To quote a recent example, Meirion and Susie Harries in *The Last Days of Innocence*, "It was almost as though Foch, as a Frenchman rather than Supreme Commander, a politician as well as a soldier, was reluctant for the Americans to distinguish themselves, content to see them bite off more than they could comfortably chew" (332). Paul F. Braim, in his book on the AEF, *The Test of Battle* (1987), declares that the idea for rerouting the American attack through the Meuse-Argonne was Douglas Haig's, and he adds: "To what extent Haig's proposal and Foch's subsequent decisions were based upon a desire to reduce the significance of the American role in the climactic campaign can only be surmised. However, the attitude of both the Allies toward the formation of an American Army is consistent with such a supposition" (83).

The implication, which has been voiced almost since the final months of the war, is that no small part of British and French thinking, once things began looking better, was premised upon preventing President Wilson from forcing through any kind of nonretributive peace treaty with Germany based on the Fourteen Points. That France's premier, Georges Clemenceau, was eminently capable of such calculation is beyond question. It ought to be added, however, that it is more likely that whatever Clemenceau and Haig may have had in mind, what Foch wanted first and foremost was to drive the Germans out of northern France as swiftly and as completely as could be done. His dealings not only with Pershing but also with Haig and Henri Petain show his determination to achieve that end, no matter what price in casualties might be necessary.

I do not fault Keegan for declining to depict Foch's demand that Pershing change his plans as part of a plot to discredit the Americans. That notion strikes me as dubious, and the insistence upon it in some quarters can even begin to approach paranoia after a time. What I object to is the almost total absence of any mechanism whatever for handling the performance of the Americans *as an army*. Because of this, Keegan is unable to deal effectively with the controversy over the use to be made of the Americans to win the war on the Western Front. Apparently he does not consider it an important issue. Perhaps not, but it certainly seemed important to the commanders on the Western Front.

Beyond doubt the Americans were clearly not prepared for what they encountered in the Meuse-Argonne, and they took extremely heavy casualties before they finally broke through towards Sedan. The fact remains that the AEF's most formidable campaign, and the widespread criticism made of Pershing's direction of it then and later, finds no place in a book of military history entitled *The First World War*.

Keegan's history focuses on World War I as a whole. The specific involvement of the United States in the war is the subject of two recent books, Meirion and Susie Harries's *The Last Days of Innocence:*

America at War 1917–1918 (1997), and Byron Farwell's *Over There: The United States in the Great War, 1917–1918* (2000). The Harries volume is the seventh book by this British couple, and, to quote from the jacket copy, "their third to focus on the effects of total war in the twentieth century." The new volume has two goals: to chronicle the American Army's experience on the Western Front, and to describe what World War I managed to do to the American psyche. Generally it is seen to have severely warped it.

Since I shall have things to criticize about the book, let me say at once that *The Last Days of Innocence* is interesting reading. It holds the reader's attention from start to finish. The authors have a gift for identifying what is controversial and dramatic and focusing upon it to vivid effect. The descriptions of the AEF's performance in battle are by far the best part of it, and the least given to what I think is the book's principal shortcoming, which is a pronounced tendency toward overdramatization.

Unhappily the talent for theatrics is sometimes allowed to overpower the plausibility of the narrative. Consider, for example, their handling of the impact upon the American Army of the decision, in late August of 1918 after the Ludendorff offensive had clearly shot its bolt, to move into a counteroffensive and to try to win the war in 1918. The controversy has already been noted above.

The facts are well known. Pershing, who was determined to get the AEF established as a separate army rather than as "cannon fodder" (the characterization is Hubert C. Johnson's in *Breakthrough!* noted earlier) for the British and French, was all set for the AEF to undertake its first offensive as an army, against the St. Mihiel salient. But shortly before jump-off time, Ferdinand Foch was persuaded by Douglas Haig—not that it took much persuading—that the Germans could be driven out of France and the war won in 1918.

Foch and his executive officer Maxime Weygand therefore showed up at AEF headquarters and proposed to Pershing that the American Army move sixty miles to the north, where it would be divided between the French army and a smaller American army under French supervision, and go into action in a concerted drive on and through the Hindenburg Line.

Pershing objected vigorously. There was an acrimonious exchange. Ultimately it was agreed that the St. Mihiel attack would go forward, after which the AEF would move northward but would not be part of the French army's attack. Instead it would take on the rugged Meuse-Argonne sector *as* an American army.

The Harrieses make the most of this episode, but in so doing they expand both the motives behind Foch's request and the alternatives available to Pershing beyond what can be justified by the known facts. Pershing had planned for the AEF to assume the main burden of the war on the Western Front not in 1918 but the year following, in 1919, they declare. The St. Mihiel salient attack was to be only the prelude to a drive that would open the way for a full-fledged, war-winning onslaught toward Metz early the following year—"Pershing's vision of glory," the Harrieses characterize it (329). At the time of Foch's request the major portion of the AEF's divisions were still untrained and unready to go into action. By conforming to the change in plans, therefore, Pershing "risked the total collapse of his command in order to support a strategy devised by the Allies that, if it succeeded, would quite possibly give them and not him the lion's share of the credit. And this in turn would make it harder for the President to exert anything but a modest influence at the peace conference. . . . In retrospect, he might seem to have betrayed his President's trust" (333–34).

What had happened, the authors contend, was that "Pershing seems to have accepted that Germany would be beaten in 1918, with or without his help, and that by 1919 there might be no war for America to win" (334). Therefore he sent largely untrained American divisions up against the waiting machine guns and artillery of the German defenders in the killing ground of the Meuse-Argonne, where they took heavy losses and were held up while elsewhere the Allies forged ahead. Pershing thus played into the hands of the British and French, who, fearful of the prestige and authority that a victorious U.S. Army would confer upon President Wilson, and determined to minimize the AEF's role, engaged in a full-scale campaign to discount the United States' contribution to the war.

Now it is quite true that no small portion of the American troops who engaged in the Meuse-Argonne campaign were insufficiently trained for the task. That their inexperience cost them far heavier casualties than would have otherwise been necessary is undeniable. It is also a fact that the Allies were unhappy at the role that Woodrow Wilson was already setting out to play in negotiations with the Germans. Nor can it be doubted that, having sustained millions of casualties in four years of desperate fighting, the British and French were less than pleased with the notion that the Johnny-come-lately Americans be credited with "winning the war."

Even so, the options that were available to Pershing that summer of 1918 are greatly exaggerated, as is the extent to which the American commander had intended to hold back his divisions for future deployment. While he is on record as aiming for the American Army to reach the stage of full participation on the Western Front in 1919, not 1918, he had by no means planned for those divisions which were sufficiently far along in their training to stay out of the fighting until then—nor indeed could he possibly have done so. With enormous expenditures of lives, resources, and capital being made by the embattled nations, and with large areas of Belgium and northern France occupied by the Germans, there could obviously be no holding back if the opportunity arose to hit the enemy hard and effectively. Pershing knew that all too well. The notion that he possessed the option of waiting in any important way until next year to join in the assault on the Germans is fanciful.

As for Foch's wanting part of Pershing's command to serve in a French army and under French direction, no theory of a deliberate, nefarious, carefully constructed Anglo-French plot to counter American influence at a future peace conference is needed to explain that. It was common knowledge that both the French and the British were eager to have American troops fighting in their ranks. After four years in which their own forces had been badly mauled and were showing decided signs of lacking zeal for more of same, quite understandably the two Allies coveted the use of the fresh, enthusiastic Americans, who had already demonstrated at Soissons and Belleau Wood that they were ready to go all-out in attacking the Germans.

Moreover, the Allies' belief that the inexperienced American officer corps was unprepared to make proper use of such fine material was not without justification, as subsequent developments in the Meuse-Argonne would show only too well. Thus the military situation alone, after four years of desperate combat on the Western Front, is quite sufficient to account for Foch's and Haig's motives, without insisting on a Franco-British plot to undercut Woodrow Wilson's role at a peace conference, with Pershing willing to sabotage his president's goals in order to take part in the final campaign.

Pershing can be criticized for not waiting to begin his attack until his more battle-experienced divisions had finished with the St. Mihiel salient and could be moved into position to spearhead the Meuse-Argonne drive, instead of leading off with his as-yet-untried divisions. It is even conceivable that as the Harrieses propose, he might have done better to call off St. Mihiel altogether, though this appears highly unrealistic to me. He can certainly be legitimately faulted for bad judgment in believing that his enthusiastic but inexperienced American Army was more capable of taking the measure of a skilled, veteran foe than was likely to be true. But to suggest that the AEF commander-in-chief could or should have held back any considerable portion of his forces until the following year in order to strengthen President Woodrow Wilson's hand at a peace conference is ridiculous.

My point is that the authors have taken an important moment in the history of the AEF, one that all commentaries on John J. Pershing's performance have rightly emphasized, and to make their retelling of it more dramatic have given it more sinister dimensions than there is proper warrant for a historian's doing. The AEF's shift from St. Mihiel to the Allied counteroffensive has been transformed into a villainous cabal by Foch, Haig, and Clemenceau designed deliberately to thwart Woodrow Wilson and force a vindictive peace upon Germany, and Pershing has been portrayed as having been hoodwinked into an arrangement that "might seem to have betrayed his President's trust." All of this makes for excellent historical melodrama, but at the cost of oversimplification and exaggeration.

The same authorial tendency toward what is stagy and theatrical is present in the depiction of life on the home front. It affects things both large and small. Let me first cite one of the latter category. In 1915, we are told, "each American aged fifteen or over drank an average of 2.4 gallons of pure alcohol a year—roughly fifty bottles of whiskey for every man, woman and teenager" (18–19). This makes for an astounding number of American citizens who were getting pie-eyed that year, the more so because by 1915 a goodly number of the states of the Union had already enacted prohibition laws.

Was every American over fifteen really averaging half a hundred bottles of Old Stepfather per annum? Only after reading the sentence a second time does it become evident that what the authors are saying is that if the total amount of alcohol consumed in a year's time were averaged out, it would then come to 2.4 gallons per inhabitant over the age of fifteen. (A gallon contains five fifths; 2.4 gallons would make twelve, not fifty fifths, or if bottled in pints, just under eighteen pints. Or is the emphasis on the adjective "pure"? If so, what proof whiskey are they talking about?) But rhetorically—"each American aged fifteen or over drank an average," etc.—the authors are proposing nothing less than a pre-1917 nation of drunks.

I mention this startling piece of nonmilitary information as an example of what I found to be a characteristic of the Harries's lively history. This is, that when reading it I repeatedly found myself thinking, "Can this really be true as stated?" In the same way, I am skeptical of the authors' depiction of the American war effort during 1918. To cite one instance, the situation on the home front a year after we entered the war is chronicled in a chapter entitled "The Will to Fight." It opens with this sentence: "Cotton and steel were not the only commodities running short by the summer of 1918; there were also worrying signs that support for the war was ebbing away" (282). We are then given an extended set of instances—strikes, resentment among ethnic groups, increases in the cost of living, inflation, profiteering including huge profits by munitions manufacturers, labor discontent, delays in fulfilling war contracts, activities of the IWW, Bolshevik agitation, lowered physical standards for the draft., etc. The chapter ends this way: "Conscripts reluctant to go to war; blacks unwilling to put national unity ahead of their own battle for equality; labor set on pursuing better pay and conditions whatever the risk to the war effort—in many ways, the country that faced the challenge to raise 100 divisions was not the one that had rallied to the President's inspiring war message little more than a year ago" (292).

I cannot question any of the specific instances of disenchantment with the war effort, difficulties in getting the job done, pursuit of private gain, etc. What is at issue is the interpretation of the significance of the examples introduced. Selective research is being used to show the United States of America swiftly turning into one large, seething mass of discontent, with the war effort in deep trouble, and just about the only people who remained committed to the defeat of the Kaiser's Germany those who were profiting from it financially.

It simply wasn't so. Certainly the people of the United States had undergone changes in the fifteen months or so between the declara-

tion of war in April of 1917 and the AEF's first offensive the following summer. The initial fervor, the excitement of the Call to Arms and
the thrilling knowledge that the Yanks Were Coming, the heady excitement of a nation going to war—"God helping her, she can do no
other"—was bound to give way to a more sobering view of what
was involved and what it meant. But I grew up among the people
who fought in that war. My father, two of my uncles, and their
friends and associates served in it, and I know how they talked about
it afterward. Moreover, I have read not a few of the numerous books
written about that time and place. I cannot credit the assertion that
in any crucial sense "support for the war was ebbing away" during
that summer of 1918.

I get the image of the authors amassing their data without fully
understanding what a great deal of it signifies, or being able to determine the extent to which the instances cited were representative
of the American scene at the time. I am far from contending that no
one but an American can write American history, or a Briton British
history. There are too many instances to the contrary. There can be
no such complaints about, for example, Byron Farwell's book. What
I am saying is that these two particular authors sometimes overstate
their material and propose sweeping conclusions.

Thus in the chapters following the one just described we are giv-
en much vivid detail about excesses of patriotic zeal, vigilante sup-
pression of free speech, widespread intolerance of dissent, instances
of hyper-Americanism, and the like. Such behavior has been described by numerous historians, and it constituted a shameful blot
on the tradition of American free speech. But one can't have it both
ways. *Either* popular support for the war effort was drastically
ebbing away, *or else* patriotic fervor was becoming excessive as the
war effort progressed. Everything that I have read indicates the latter. As Henry F. May wrote in his study of American intellectual life
in the period 1912–1917, *The End of American Innocence* (1959), "The
response to Wilson's speech [calling for a declaration of war] was a
great outpouring of energy and sacrifice and then, after a few
months of curious calm, a mighty outburst of emotion. Idealism and
Utopianism about the war went beyond all limits, and so, despite
Wilson's warnings, did hatred" (38).

I am not suggesting any attempt at misrepresentation on the authors' part. It is rather that when writing their chapter about what

was going wrong with the war effort in the summer of 1918, they were concerned with making that point as emphatically and as dramatically as possible. Then when they turned next to showing instances of super-patriotism, they set out to dramatize that point with equal zeal. That any contradiction might be involved, that the complexity of the phenomenon being described might be such that a hasty grouping of dramatic episodes arranged by topics might not get at the underlying nature of what was happening, did not occur to them.

Moreover, their thesis—that becoming involved in the Great War wrought catastrophic wounds upon the national psyche—is overdone, and demonstrates some naïveté about the complex nature of American history between the Civil War and the election of Woodrow Wilson. The authors were exuberantly engaged in developing a thesis that might have caused even an Arnold Toynbee or R. H. Tawney to think twice. Their approach does indeed make for exciting narrative, suspense, etc. But it is not an altogether reliable recipe for writing sound political, social, or military history.

To repeat, they are best on the Western Front fighting itself. Their depiction of the Americans at Belleau Wood, the Marne, and Soissons is excellent, and the extended account of the Argonne offensive, the chaos in the rear, the holdup at the Kriemhilde Position, and the role of General Hunter Liggett in the reorganization and successful advance of the U.S. First Army is presented vividly and clearly. It's when the authors leave the fighting and get into the political maneuvering that they run into trouble.

Byron Farwell has written more than a dozen books, the majority of them on English military history in the late nineteenth and early twentieth centuries, but more recently two on the American Civil War. Like Keegan and the Harrieses, he too is British, but has lived and worked in the United States for some years. *Over There: The United States in the Great War, 1917–1918* has no ruling thesis. He seeks to describe what happened when a populous and potentially powerful nation, which however was almost totally unprepared militarily, set out to raise and equip a large army to fight a war against a powerful foe four thousand miles from home, and what happened to that army when it went into battle.

Farwell offers us relatively little about the problems of command, and a great deal about the experience as it impacted upon the troops engaged in the fighting. Thus for example he does not have much to say about the constant pressure being applied to Pershing to let the Americans arriving overseas be used as replacements in the British armies—although he does chronicle the role that those divisions which did fight under British and French command played in the fighting.

Neither does he concern himself at much length with the motives behind the dispute over transferring the American operations from St. Mihiel to the Meuse-Argonne—which the Harrieses make into high drama, involving a sinister effort by the Allies to undercut Woodrow Wilson's influence in the forthcoming peace conference. The confrontation between Pershing and Foch is essentially presented as being over whether the American forces were to be divided, and half of them placed under French direction. That the U.S. divisions opening the Meuse-Argonne drive were largely untested and without adequate training is made clear—though not that it was by accepting Foch's timetable that Pershing was forced to use those divisions rather than the more experienced "blooded" units that had fought at St. Mihiel.

Farwell's depiction of the Meuse-Argonne campaign is in terms of the experience of those who were there and the ordeal they underwent. It is excellently done. It does not attempt to provide much of a sense of the design of the attack as planned, what happened to efforts to bring coordination and tactical direction to its execution, and why the elements of the design did not work out. But it gives a vivid picture of what the fighting was like, and what was involved in going up against an entrenched and skilled German army that still had a great deal of fight left in it. He makes very good use of secondary sources—memoirs, wartime correspondence, postwar descriptions by individuals. Private Charles MacArthur, Captain Harry S. Truman, Colonel Wild Bill Donovan, Chaplain Francis P. Duffy of the Fighting Sixty-ninth, and numerous others have their say.

The near-incredible human achievement of creating a fighting and ultimately victorious army out of next to nothing is not neglected, nor is the waste, inefficiency, and ugliness that went along with the task. There can be no question that getting the nation onto a war footing took far too long, that the mobilization of America's industrial resources left much to be desired, and that the vaunted American "know-how" failed in important respects to deliver the goods in time for the AEF to use them.

For all the chaos and mismanagement and suffering, there was also humor, and Farwell doesn't mind using it. Thus we learn that efforts to clean up the red light districts in American cities in order to safeguard the health and welfare of the mobilized troops training nearby were not always successful; in Kansas City, for example, "12th Avenue was known as Woodrow Wilson Avenue because it offered 'a piece at any price.'" To enable Americans to cope with a foreign language "the YMCA published a pamphlet with such helpful French expressions as, 'I should very much like to see the periscope of a submarine,' 'Do not stick your head above the trench,' and 'I have pawned my watch'" (136). The Harrieses also cite these (139). And so on.

The War to End All Wars, as the conflict was briefly titled, ended in disillusion. My father's Victory Medal calls it The Great War for Civilization. Which perhaps it was, though it left civilization in a worse mess than it found it. It was followed by confusion, boom-and-bust, worldwide economic depression, the rise of totalitarianism, and the far more terrible war of 1939–1945. Thereafter came the Cold War, together with various smaller conflicts, and only now, eight decades and more after the shooting ceased on the Western Front, have things tended to settle down—although as John Keegan notes, the ethnic and national tensions in the Balkans that set off the fighting in 1914 are again active.

At one point during the First World War, Winston Churchill upset the poet Siegfried Sassoon very much with the remark that war was the natural state of mankind. On the evidence of the century just past, it would be difficult to quarrel with him. On the other hand, if there is any hope for the future it would appear to lie in our being able to throttle those natural instincts—a process which is known as civilization. Yet if the history of the past hundred years shows us anything, it is that the oft-voiced bromide that it takes two to make a fight is not and never has been true. A single aggressor willing to take long risks is all that has ever been needed.

6

Literature and the Great War

(1992)

The newspaper in Scotland, where we were vacationing this past summer, contained a lengthy feature story, telling of the death of the writer's youthful uncle seventy-five years earlier, on July 1, 1916, the first day of the Battle of the Somme. Meanwhile the television news was showing sequences from the current crisis in the Balkans, involving Serbia, Slovenia, Bosnia, Herzegovina, place names that had not figured in international discourse since the summer that the archduke was assassinated.

Bosnia? Herzegovina? My god! To remember the outbreak of the Great War—World War I—and the Battle of the Somme with any clarity, one would have to be in one's mid-eighties. And to be old enough to have served in the AEF—the American Expeditionary Force—one would be in one's nineties. Of the almost five million Americans who were in the armed forces in 1917–1918, according to the *World Almanac,* fewer than ninety thousand were still alive last year. Xerxes of Persia, gazing down from a hilltop upon the vast array of men and ships engaged in crossing the Hellespont, is said by Herodotus to have wept at the thought that in a hundred years not one person of all the mighty host lying below him would still be alive. "Pack up your troubles in your old kit bag and smile, smile, smile!"

It is said that writing about wars customarily adheres to a pattern. For a decade or so after a war ends, there is much reader interest. The major figures write their memoirs, and the returned veterans are eager to read about their own experience in the larger context of the fighting. Then topical interest wanes, and for several decades most books on the subject attract little notice and only professional military people and a few historians continue to concern themselves with what happened.

When the former rank-and-file of the armies and navies reach late middle age, retire from their civilian jobs and vocations, and begin looking back, a resurgence of interest develops. The fact, so long taken for granted, that one was involved when young in an extraordinary and momentous activity, given a uniform and transported to strange places and, if sent into combat made to participate in shocking events and endure all manner of discomforts and ordeals, becomes in later life an occasion for wonder. The memoirs again appear in droves, this time not by the major figures but by the onetime rank-and-file. Meanwhile passions have receded, the military historians revaluate command performances, and the battles and campaigns, strategy and tactics, come in for renewed and more nearly objective scrutiny. Thereafter interest in and study of a war becomes a matter of pure historical involvement alone.

In the instance of World War I, however, there *was* no "third stage," or at most a very muted version of it, for during the 1950s and 1960s, when the veterans of 1914–1918 had reached their time of retrospection, the Second World War had intervened—a greater and more far-reaching event (especially for the United States) with more momentous and terrible consequences. The results of 1914–1918 had proved to be neither decisive nor lasting, and from a standpoint of getting books written and published, few persons there were who wished to read about the Somme, Ypres, Tannenburg, Jutland, Passchendaele, and the Meuse-Argonne.

So the Great War's veterans went to their graves without their latter-day revival; no fifty-years-later festivals of onetime mortal foes shaking hands across the formerly muddy and louse-infested trenches, no sentimental journeys to St. Mihiel and Flanders Field, no reenactments of Zeppelin raids or mustard-gas attacks. Behind one's thought of Paul von Hindenburg and his *pickelhaube* lay one's consciousness of Adolf Hitler, the swastika, and the gas ovens. When Scott Fitzgerald had his narrator in *The Great Gatsby* refer to the Great War as a "delayed Teutonic migration," he was essentially correct. Thwarted in 1918, the Fatherland thereafter dropped all pretense of being civilized, and reverted to the diplomatic tactics and social attitudes of Attila the Hun.

Chronologically speaking, a scholar writing about 1914–1918 today bears much the same relationship to General John J. Pershing and the AEF as Theodore Roosevelt did to Oliver Hazard Perry and the sail-powered navy when he was writing *A Naval History of the War of 1812* in the early 1880s. He can be objective enough about the performance of American arms to describe ineptitude without apology or alibi. It is quite possible for a historian like Colonel Rod Paschall to point out that despite the extremely low number of American casualties in the Great War as compared with those of England, France, and Germany, the deaths and wounding suffered by the AEF were extraordinarily high in relation to the period of actual involvement in combat and the number of troops engaged (*The Defeat of Imperial Germany, 1917–1918,* 1989). American leadership had failed to benefit from the four-year experience of the British and French on the Western Front, and was basing U.S. tactics on advance by concentrated rifle fire, as if the machine guns hadn't discouraged that approach for several years.

At Belleau Wood in 1918 the U.S. Marine brigade was sent charging right into the teeth of machine-gun fire, advancing four deep in human-wave attacks after the fashion of 1914, or, for that matter, of Grant's army at Cold Harbor in 1864. German and British observers, seeing the American dead fallen in serried rows in the Argonne Forest, expressed admiration for their courage and severe criticism of their tactical leadership. (American casualties totaled 364,800, as compared with more than nine million Russians killed, wounded, missing, or captured, six million French, seven million Germans, seven million Austro-Hungarians, three million English and Commonwealth troops, and two million Italians.)

Colonel Paschall's revaluation of what happened during the final two years of the Great War involves a marked upgrading of the leadership on the Western Front. He does not see such figures as Douglas Haig, who commanded the British armies from 1916 onward, as stupid, unimaginative, unfeeling old martinets who knew no better than repeatedly to dispatch entire brigades and divisions of men over the top and straight into the face of machine guns and artillery barrages. The offensive tactics that early in World War II sent the German *blitzkrieg* hurtling through France and the Low Countries and almost trapped the British at Dunkirk, and that in 1944 and 1945 enabled Eisenhower's invading forces to hurl Hitler's armies back across the Rhine, were all developed by the generals of the Great War, who, however, possessed neither the resources nor the equipment to employ them successfully. In Paschall's summation, "in reality, most World War II leaders simply repeated what they had seen implemented under the direction of Foch, Pétain, Haig, Sims, Trenchard, and Ludendorff. There would not be much new in World War II; the changes were already in motion during 1917" (230).

Yet if the war of 1939–1945 was vaster, more destructive, and more far-reaching in scope than that of 1914–1918, it is nonetheless true that in terms of cultural shock and the imaginative impact on life in the Western world, the Great War came on with greater and more decisive impress. There were numerous reasons for this. Except for the American Civil War, and then only in the southern states, it had been a full century since an extended all-out war involving large segments of the civilian population had been fought. During that time the available weaponry had benefited enormously in deadliness from the Industrial Revolution. A greatly more destructive and more impersonal kind of warfare, coming as it did after a hundred years of relative peace in Europe, happened to a population that by 1914 was constituted largely of citizens who were literate, who could read and compare versions of what was told to them, and who voted. It came after a century of material improvement and prosperity, which was paralleled by a political and philosophical idealism that called for things to get better and better, and that elevated love of country to the status of belief in God and devotion to Truth and Beauty.

The shock of trench warfare—the appalling, almost suicidal requirements of going over the top against emplaced machine guns, mass slaughter of long-range artillery fired by unseen opponents, the huge scale on which war was being waged—was mind-searing. As the Western Front settled into a condition of bloody stalemate, the conditions under which men were made to live and to fight seemed the antithesis of what civilized existence was supposed to be. After it became obvious that there would be no quick solution to the ordeal, the moral and ethical assumptions developed during generations of peace and of seeming material and social progress received an abrupt check. The ensuing disillusionment, coming as it did so swiftly and catastrophically, called into question the validity of the basic ideals under which the Western world had supposedly been functioning. The gap between belief and actuality, between patriotic faith and the requirements of trench warfare, took on the dimensions of an abyss.

Paul Fussell, in his widely praised *The Great War and Modern Memory* (1975), has described and interpreted the impress made by the shock of the Great War upon English modes of thought and expression, which in turn, as Fussell demonstrates, influenced American attitudes. Such impress went far beyond the war itself; it permeated, and has continued to permeate, the Western world's ways of seeing the human condition. The key concept for Fussell in his consideration of the impact of 1914–1918 is irony: "I am saying that there seems to be one dominating form of modern understanding; that it is essentially ironic; and that it originates largely in the application of mind and memory to the events of the Great War" (35).

The ironic vision was by no means invented in late 1914 and 1915. Fussell opens with a consideration of Thomas Hardy's poems, which in their perception of incongruity presage the response of poets both English and American to what would soon follow. He then proceeds to demonstrate how the imagery of trench warfare, bombardment, wounds, "combat fatigue," futility, disbelief in the reality of any kind of victory that would be commensurate with the human cost of achieving it, juxtaposed with the patriotic rhetoric, official pronouncements, and pious ideality, suffuses modern consciousness. Fussell discusses the writings of Wilfred Owen, Siegfried Sassoon, Robert Graves, Edmund Blunden, and other British authors; he then develops the continuity of attitude in such authors as Anthony Burgess, Joseph Heller, and Thomas Pynchon.

The Great War and Modern Memory is a thesis book: it develops a psychological point and argues for it. Occasionally the thesis becomes omnivorous—for example, trenches being dug in threes (forward, support, reserve) and other tripartite divisions decreed by the nature of the Great War supposedly fed myth and legend with particular appropriateness. I suspect that just as convincing an argu-

ment could be developed for just about any war, any historical period, or any low single-digit number; it was an Ancient Mariner, not a
British tommy, who, like a poor-caliber infielder, stoppeth one of
three. Yet Fussell's basic thesis—that the impact of the trench warfare of 1914–1918 upon a popular and literary imagination unprepared for its magnitude, impersonal nature, bloodiness, and
animality was both devastating and enduring—is imaginatively advanced and soundly demonstrated.

Of a very different nature, but concerned with the literary and cultural ramifications of the same historical event, is Samuel Hynes's *A
War Imagined: The First World War and English Culture* (1991). Hynes
has long since shown himself to be our major student of Edwardian
and Georgian English letters. He writes with the authority of the
scholar and the insight of the critic, and does not so much develop
and argue points as reveal and identify patterns. In *A War Imagined*
he examines the way that English writers and painters, as well as
sculptors and musicians, dealt with, depicted, and were affected by
the First World War, from its beginnings through to the Armistice,
and then the postwar years culminating in the British General Strike
of 1926.

Hynes is at pains to make clear that the notion that the coming of
war to Great Britain in 1914 brought a sudden end to a stable, progressive, comfortably ordered and civilized society is a considerable
oversimplification—a myth prompted by nostalgia. Ireland was
close to a state of civil war at the time; the suffragettes were turning
violent; trade unions were threatening a general strike: "a civil war,
a sex war, and a class war: in the spring of 1914 these were all foreseen in England's immediate future" (7). On the cultural front the advocates of futurism and vorticism were proclaiming an all-out attack
upon the Edwardian "Establishment."

When the Great War erupted, Hynes points out, it was identified
by older figures such as Edmund Gosse as a potential "disinfectant
that would cleanse the present—and not simply present art, but all
of 'our' self-indulgent, hedonistic, luxurious habits." Thus Gosse, he
says, "could be positive about the situation in France: war would pu-
rify and cleanse; war was good for England" (12). Surveying a wide
spectrum of writings about the war by various hands on various cultural levels, Hynes shows how "the war against Germany rapidly
became a war against Modernism" (64); war was being declared

against the avant-garde. Denunciations of everything German—including German music, German thought, German science, German romanticism—were rampant. Yet as Hynes notes, so much of what was being repudiated had equally been English, and the result was not only a diminishment of English culture but "a further widening of that gap between the past and the present, that breach in the perceived continuity of history, which was the war's most striking legacy to the world after the war" (78).

Yet there *was* dissent, Hynes shows: the Bloomsbury group, among others, were dissenters even in the early years of the war. What happened, Hynes declares, is that "a divided culture began to emerge: on the one hand, the war culture—patriotic, restrictive, and 'official,' and on the other, that conflux of opposing faiths—the artists, pacifists, women, and radical Christians who constituted such opposition to the war as there was" (96).

The turning point in the way that English writers and artists depicted the war and that at least a segment of the general public viewed it, Hynes says, came in 1916, mainly following the huge losses in the Somme offensive. Patriotic idealism, Rupert Brooke–fashion ("If I should die, think only this of me, / that there's some corner of a foreign field / that is forever England . . . "), gave way to a considerably more sardonic view of the waging of war:

> Protests against it began to be heard, both from civilians in high places and from serving soldiers, and a new English war art began to emerge that uttered its own protest simply by recording a new trench reality. That new reality had to do with details that had largely been left out of previous war art: the devastated earth, the corpses, and the wounded—blinded men, gassed men, crippled men, mad men, men with self-inflicted wounds. But it also had to do with feelings that were new to the art of this war: pity and compassion for its victims, anger and hatred for non-combatants. (187)

Hynes traces the forms and shapes of this new art, much of it by and for soldiers, in a series of detailed chapters that authoritatively survey work by representative writers and artists. The war effort continued, and so did the efforts of those who would suppress dissent on the grounds that "pacifists were refusing to serve in the army, and were persuading others to refuse; advocates of a negotiated peace were weakening the nation's resolve to fight on to total victory; and a permissive, un-English decadence in high places was corrupting English society" (217).

By 1918 what was to be England's "postwar modernism" was beginning to emerge, in the writings of returning soldiers, the Bloomsbury group, dissenters such as D. H. Lawrence, and the like. What had resulted was a sense of deep discontinuity. A work such as Lytton Strachey's *Eminent Victorians,* for example, seemingly had nothing whatever to do with the Great War; yet its demolition of Victorianism was a demonstration that "History was not a story of liberal progress, with a continuous happy ending; the ending was the war. And so the story would have to be re-told to accommodate that disaster" (244–45). The past was dead, the future all but unimaginable. If English society was to be reconstructed, there could be no postwar return to what in Edwardian England was believed to be the Good, the True, and the Beautiful.

Hynes examines the various models being proposed. He identifies five distinct postwar clusters of literary activity: (1) "The Old Men," the surviving late Victorian elders such as Gosse, Sir Henry Newbolt, etc., who saw the war as a continuation of their prewar values; (2) "Edwardians," such as H. G. Wells and Arnold Bennett, who strove to stay up-to-date but were disturbed and apprehensive about what had been lost and what survived; (3) "The Pre-War Avant-Garde," such as Wyndham Lewis, Ezra Pound, etc., who had declared war on conservative art back before the Great War began, but whose formulations for doing so had thoroughly disintegrated; (4) "The War Generation," or "Lost Generation," including both the surviving soldiers of what had been a massacre of the upper and middle classes, and those who had stayed at home but were likewise disoriented, confused, groping for order—Huxley, Eliot, Muir, Lawrence, Middleton Murry, Woolf, etc.; and (5) "The Post-War Generation," growing into adulthood as and after the war ended—Evelyn Waugh, Ronald Firbank, and so on. The working members of all these groups had to deal with a greatly changed English society and world, marked by a sense of radical discontinuity. Their responses were of numerous kinds.

It would be impractical to attempt further to summarize Hynes's summarization of post-1918 literary England, which is explicit, succinct, and informed; but I cannot refrain from quoting one passage. In it he is looking at the writers who did not serve in the war but who set the tone for dealing with what had happened:

> Eliot and Pound, Virginia Woolf and Lawrence—these are major Modernists, writers whose works define what is most valued in English writings of the 1920s. None of them had any experience of the war, and none wrote a war novel or a war poem in the customary sense of those terms. But they did something more interesting, and perhaps more important: they assimilated the war into their writing, both as concept and as form, made it a part of their idea of history, and of reality. The version of history that they shared is the post-war version; it renders recent history as discontinuous and fragmented, civilization as ruined, the past as lost. . . . Their writings contain no battle scenes, no heroes, and no victories; they pick up from the war only the dominating negative themes—the death of civilization and the loss of Eden, and the negative characters—the damaged victims, and the tyrannous Old Men. And they construct out of this heap of broken images the forms of the history of their own time. (348)

Has anyone ever put that particular point better?

The important literature dealing with the war itself, Hynes notes, did not begin to appear until late in the decade. He sees the ten-day British General Strike of 1926 as the event that culturally, intellectually, and psychologically "ended" the Great War itself. The strike, which came close to paralyzing the workings of British society, was described and thought of *as* a war against society and, when it was broken, as a victory. Like the war, the strike had forced another gap in the continuity of history, Hynes says, and when it was over the events of 1914–1918 were sufficiently distanced in the imagination so that new ideas could now find expression. The Myth of the Great War—that it betrayed the ideals of the past, turned men into victims of an inhuman machine so that they fought for no cause, destroyed the idea of progress, civilization, England, and left the survivors to live among a heap of ruins—now took form in prose, poetry, painting, movies. "The history of English art and thought in the Twenties," Hynes declares, "is a record of attempts to reconstruct history and values, and so build a new culture out of the broken images made by the war. Only at the end of that decade was the war itself remade, the vast loss described and mythologized, in the prose narratives that became the war-book canon" (459).

The effect of all this upon the 1930s is not Hynes's story. He does, however, note that it was this myth of the war, inherited by the next generation and intensified by the Great Depression, that made the 1930s what they were, including pacifism, political activism, proto-fascism, and the defensive drawing-in when the Western democracies were confronted by the rise of totalitarianism. When World War II came, those who marched off to fight it "would go without dreams of glory, expecting nothing except suffering, boredom and perhaps death—not cynically, but without illusions, because they remembered a war: not the Great War itself, but the Myth that had been made of it" (467–68).

A War Imagined, it seems to me, has taken a complex cultural entity—the literature written in England over the course of almost two decades, as well as the visual arts, music, film—and examined it in terms of its relationship to a mammoth, near-catastrophic political and social event, the Great War and the decade following it. Hynes has enabled us to see and to understand what the relationship was and what it meant, both for the creative work and the culture from which it rose. For a literary historian who is also a fine critic, I can think of few more useful undertakings.

To my knowledge no one has successfully brought off a similar study of American literature with anything of the scope and range of Sam Hynes's book. Yet, as a British critic noted some years ago, despite the brevity of our involvement, the Great War's impact on the American literary imagination was extraordinarily penetrating and pervasive. And perhaps this is less paradoxical than might appear, for as has often been pointed out, our entrance into the conflict in 1917 ended what until then had been not merely a geographical but a psychological isolation from the Old World. Coinciding as it did with the formal disappearance of the western frontier, the arrival of American troops in France wrote a formal conclusion to the Emersonian dream of regeneration in nature and the creation of a new man free of the bondage and toils of the European past. As one historian, Henry W. May, entitled his study of late nineteenth- and early twentieth-century American society, it was truly *The End of Amer-*

ican Innocence. (To be sure, all of our best novelists—Cooper, Hawthorne, Melville, James, Clemens—had long since discounted any such possibility, but naive optimism dies hard, and three thousand miles of ocean and an open frontier had constituted a powerful temptation.) In any event, whatever the causes, the literary response to the Great War was as marked, and as morose, among American as among English authors.

I want to turn back briefly to Paul Fussell's observation that irony has been the predominant mode of the twentieth-century literary imagination, and that the Great War has significantly to do with that. Has anyone ever thought of the critical approach known as the New Criticism as constituting an oblique response to the War of 1914–1918? Sam Hynes suggests as much, when he cites Laura Riding's and Robert Graves's *A Survey of Modernist Poetry*, published in 1927, as not only the first book to use the term *modernist* to identify avant-garde writing, but "the first to demonstrate a new critical method for dealing with Modernist texts—the method that would come to be called 'The New Criticism'" (419).

There is a distinct and specific biographical link. In the early and mid-1920s, Laura Riding, then living in New York, was an honorary member of the Nashville Fugitives at that time, while John Crowe Ransom was corresponding regularly with Graves about poetry and poetics. (The story of the visit of Riding to Nashville in December 1924 is among the more piquant episodes in southern letters; as Ransom wrote to Allen Tate somewhat later, she "did not realize that we had already established our respective personal relationships on satisfactory and rather final bases, and that we were open to literary relationships but not to personal" [*Selected Letters of John Crowe Ransom,* 151].) Riding did have an involvement with—as might be guessed—Tate, who at one point was insisting that she and Hart Crane were the most important talents of the decade. It was Ransom who introduced Riding to Graves, who was taken with one of her poems, with momentous results. More important, of course, was the intellectual milieu in which these writers, who would soon develop in more formal fashion the method known as the New Criticism, existed. They absorbed Eliot's poetry and prose. They knew I. A. Richards's *Science and Poetry* and, later, *Practical Criticism.*

In *The Sun Also Rises* Hemingway has Jake Barnes and Bill Gorton discourse upon the fashionable employment of "irony and pity" in

then-current critical parlance. As noted earlier, the use of ironic discourse goes considerably further back in time than the events on the
Marne and the Somme; in First Samuel the women of Israel are reported as remarking to Saul: "Saul hath slain his thousands, and
David his ten thousands." But there can be little question that the
chasm between civilized ideal and human actuality that the impact
of the Great War laid bare shocked the literary imagination into a
suspicion of abstraction and a preoccupation with what was tangi-
ble and concrete in language. Hemingway's oft-cited remarks in *A
Farewell to Arms* about words such as "glory, honor, courage and hal-
low" appearing "obscene beside the concrete names of villages, the
numbers of roads, the names of villages, the numbers of regiments
and the dates" are to the point.

The New Criticism's penchant for irony and paradox was, after all,
no more or less than an insistence upon protecting the language of
poetry from tenuous, gauzy affirmations and vague claims to un-
earned significance, to safeguard the right of the poetic imagination
to be taken seriously. The New Critics insisted that what was being
asserted be carefully *looked* at; they wanted the poem to count for
something, to matter: they wanted the reader to be given the opportunity to take part in the transaction, and not merely be manipulated by verbal and rhetorical sleight-of-hand.

Thus the instructional classic of the movement, Cleanth Brooks
and Robert Penn Warren's *Understanding Poetry,* defines "irony" in
the glossary to the 1950 edition in these words: "An ironical statement indicates a meaning contrary to the one it professes to give . . ."
and Brooks and Warren go on to remark that "irony, along with un-
derstatement (in which there is a discrepancy, great or small, between what is *actually* said and what *might* be said), is a device of In-
direct Method. . . . That is, the poet does not present his meaning
abstractly or explicitly, but depends on the reader's capacity to develop implications imaginatively" (690). Paradox was "a statement
which seems on the surface contradictory, but which involves an element of truth" (691).

The implicit relationship between such doctrine and the experience of 1914–1918 can be seen in a comment made in the introduction to *Understanding Poetry,* in which Brooks and Warren, in
warning against the manipulation of human emotions through unexamined verbal associations, depose as follows: "Advertising, of

course, raises the question in an extreme form. Advertisers naturally are not content to rest on a statement of fact, whether such a statement is verifiable or not. They will attempt to associate the attitude toward a certain product with an attitude toward beautiful women, little children, or grey-haired mothers; they will appeal to snobbishness, vanity, *patriotism, religion, and morality" (xli,* italics mine).

In the same way, the insistence upon the primacy of the actual poetic text, and the importance of anchoring one's consideration of the poem in the language of the text itself, is surely the response to a cultural experience in which the public rhetoric employed to interpret what was happening on the Western Front, and the visceral, physical, and mental ordeal of human beings inhabiting trenches, produced an appalling discrepancy of meaning. The New Criticism was, in this sense, an effort to rectify the damage insofar as reading poetry was involved.

To return to the larger issue, I recall it being remarked, with some regret, when well into World War II, that unlike the Great War, there were no good American popular songs being written and sung about the event—no "Pack Up Your Troubles," "Keep the Home Fires Burning," "Over There," not even a "Mademoiselle from Armentieres" or "You're In the Army Now." The virtuosi of Tin Pan Alley were grinding out the pop tunes, but it was without exception wretched stuff. Certainly there were obvious reasons—the lack of novelty about the experience, a larger public sophistication, the awareness this time of what we were in for, and so on.

What it came down to, however, was the fact that, in having to do what it was doing, the generation that engaged in World War II didn't see a great deal to sing happy or inspiring songs about. Generally it made do with the old ones, or else chose songs that had nothing to do with war and fighting. And that, it strikes me, was all in all a good thing. Clearly it had nothing to do with morale, civilian or military, which from Pearl Harbor through V-J Day was resolute. But it showed that while engaging in a war might be necessary (as indeed the defeat of Nazi and Imperial Japanese militarism was), there was nothing romantic or ennobling about doing so, but principally a distressing business of killing and surviving. Heroism there could be, and was, but it was heroism on the job, not on a football field or in the lists at Ashby la Zouch. One can only hope that what these wars taught will continue to be remembered when all the actual participants in them have disappeared, and that our literature will allow us to forget neither the hideousness nor, even despite the frustrations of Ypres, the Somme, or, in World War II, Anzio Beach, the bitter necessity.

7

T. R.

(2005)

On a May morning a few years ago, a friend and I watched from the shore as the aircraft carrier USS *Theodore Roosevelt*, back with its battle group from a six-month tour of duty in the eastern Mediterranean and the Arabian Gulf, eased to its berth at the Norfolk Naval Base. Thousands of people were on hand, a band was playing away, and a multicolored barrage of crepe ribbon streamed out on all sides as eight tugboats shoved it toward the wharf.

White-uniformed sailors and blue-clad marines stood at parade rest along the rims of its angled flight deck. Nuclear powered, with a complement of 6,000 officers and crew, displacing 91,209 tons, 1,089 feet long and 164 feet in beam, its engines producing 280,000 horsepower, the *T. R.* was a formidable fighting machine.

Beyond the naval base lay Hampton Roads, where not quite ninety years earlier Theodore Roosevelt had sent the Great White Fleet off around the world, and twenty months afterward, as one of the final acts of his presidency, had greeted the fleet upon its return. On that day in 1909, twenty-six warships had fired a simultaneous twenty-one-gun salute, then each of twenty battleships individually repeated the cannonade.

Had T. R. been on hand in 1997 for the return of his nuclear-powered namesake from the Mideast, surely he would have been "deelighted!" He enjoyed the display of military and naval might and the tumult and excitement of gala public doings. He liked to be at the center of whatever was happening, and took pride in his constitutional role as commander-in-chief of the armed forces. It would have deeply gratified him to know that, nearly a century after he left office, his name would remain an appropriate designation for a floating icon of American military prowess.

Assuredly our twenty-sixth American president is far from being forgotten. On the contrary, of late there has been positively a resurgence of historical interest in him. Kathleen Dalton's new biography, *Theodore Roosevelt: A Strenuous Life* (2002), is one of the best of at least half a dozen studies to appear within the past ten years. The year before, Edmund Morris published *Theodore Rex* (2001), covering T. R.'s White House years, the second in what when completed seems likely will be the definitive three-volume assessment. Louis Auchincloss has written a brief, unremarkable biographical summary, *Theodore Roosevelt*, in a series entitled American Presidents (2002). H. W. Brands's notable biography, *T. R.: The Last Romantic*, appeared in 1997, and Edward J. Renehan, Jr.,'s *The Lion's Pride: Theodore Roosevelt and His Family in Peace and War* in 1998. David McCullough's *Mornings on Horseback* (1981), an account of T. R.'s younger days, has been reissued with a new introduction (2001). T. R. plays a commanding role in Warren Zimmerman's *First Great Triumph: How Five Americans Made Their Country a World Power* (2002), and in James Chace's *1912* (2004). He has recently been the subject of a multi-episode television documentary.

A selection of his writings, *The Man in the Arena: Selected Writings of Theodore Roosevelt: A Reader,* has been "edited " by Bryan M. Thomsen (2003). I place the word in quotation marks because the compilation is distinguished by the absence of any introductory and explanatory material whatever to set the context of the excerpts chosen. The "select bibliography" of "critical/biographical works on Roosevelt" is a farce.

The historical reputations of political figures tend to fluctuate in approximate response to the needs of the generations that come after them. T. R.'s fame has had its ups and downs. During the first decade of the twentieth century it was at perihelion. In the years of

Woodrow Wilson's presidency and the Great War there was a falling off. In the 1930s and 1940s the renown of his fifth cousin, Franklin Delano Roosevelt, came to eclipse his own. In the middle decades of the century, as the nation was coming to grips with its failures in civil rights, the status of women, and the "military-industrial complex," the tendency among historians has been to view T. R.'s administration as having been longer on rhetoric than on substance.

In recent years that verdict has undergone substantial alteration, for his specific accomplishments as president seem less important than his imaginative impact upon the office. T. R. is increasingly seen as in effect the creator of the modern American presidency, who did much to shape the federal government into an active force for domestic social and economic betterment and a major participant in international affairs.

When one century ends and another begins, we are prompted to look back at the last time it happened. During the early 1900s, when T. R. was "Theodore Rex," as Henry James once styled him, he was by all odds the dominant, most memorable figure in American public life. He was war hero, historian, conservationist, outdoorsman, reformer, trust-buster, advocate of the strenuous life, moralist, pundit, and above all, gifted politico. He had intelligence, executive ability, and extraordinary energy, qualities that when they intersect in a politician can create a notable commotion. The assassination of William McKinley in 1901 may have put him into the White House several years earlier than anticipated, but to the extent that anything is ever inevitable in politics, in retrospect surely T. R.'s eventual advent was.

He was, and as Kathleen Dalton declares in the introduction to her biography a century later, remains, "America's most fascinating president" (*Theodore Roosevelt,* 12). The widespread public affection he earned in his day still holds. So does the awareness of his shortcomings and absurdities. What we remember above all is the excitement and ebullience of T. R.'s personality. He was good copy. Morris quotes one newspaperman who during a two-week presidential vacation in Yellowstone National Park commented that like Old Faithful geyser, T. R. could be counted on for "intermittent but continuous spouting" (*Theodore Rex,* 221).

After his second term was over, T. R. remarked that the likelihood of his being remembered as one of the great presidents was diminished by the fact that there was no war or major crisis during his time of leadership. This may have been true; if so, certainly T. R. managed to overcome that apparent handicap. In terms of the talents that he brought to the job, however, it is more likely that the timing of his ascendancy was strikingly auspicious.

The nation was, in George Mowry's description, somewhat tardily confronting "the amazing number of domestic and foreign problems spawned by the great industrial, urban, and population changes of the late nineteenth century" (*The Era of Theodore Roosevelt* [1958], xv). The decade of his presidency marked the onset of the Progressive Era. In the face of enormous corporate wealth and economic combinations of unprecedented power and influence, there was a growing consensus that the federal government would have to intervene to protect and sustain the welfare of small businesses, working people, farmers, ordinary citizens in general.

Moreover, with the War of 1898 the United States became a major player on the world scene. Expansion was in the air. The first decisive steps were taken whereby our country began to move into its present-day role of international leadership. What happened in our era of imperial adventuring—which, it must be said, was at no time entirely whole-souled—was not always either admirable or lovely. Yet in retrospect it would be difficult to see it as other than inevitable. As Warren Zimmerman writes in *First Great Triumph*, "It was in large part because of America's actions as a great power that the twentieth century was not the 'Century of the Third Reich' or the 'Century of the Glorious Victory of World Communism'" (475).

If so, most of all it was T. R. who steered the nation toward that role. Congress by its very nature could not provide that kind of direction; the initiative must come from the White House. Being by instinct and preference an activist, T. R. was exactly the person needed to furnish it. We think of his presidency in terms of *doing:* prying the Isthmus of Panama loose from Colombia and digging the Panama Canal; prosecuting the Northern Securities, Standard Oil, and sugar trusts; outlawing rebates to powerful shippers and providing the first really effective railroad rate regulation; forcing through a Pure Food and Drug Act; placing the federal government squarely on the side of conservation of natural resources; negotiating a treaty to end the Russo-Japanese War; sending the battle fleet around the world.

To change people's assumptions, including those of their elected representatives in Congress, about what was proper and appropriate for the president and the federal government to do and to be, it was necessary for T. R. to appeal directly to the voters. Like no president before him he knew how to mobilize public opinion and bring it to bear on what as he developed his legislative agenda became an ever more reluctant Congress. In dramatizing the issues of the day, he thereby dramatized himself. To quote Mowry again, paraphrasing T. R., "The country was moving, and Roosevelt, being a good democratic politician, was ready to move with it and guide it in the ways of moderation, expediency, and righteousness" (223). So T. R. assured a friend.

"Moderation" is hardly the word that the northeastern financial and business community would have chosen to describe his approach to his job. Starting out as a conservative Republican, and at all times convinced that he was striving to protect the country from anarchy and revolution by making government responsive to the needs of the have-nots, he grew steadily more radical. By the time of his final Annual Message to Congress, he was calling for government control of railroads, workmen's compensation and employer liability laws, an eight-hour working day for government employees, inheritance and income taxes, an end to court injunctions against striking workers, and centralization of power in the office of the presidency. He even pointed out that when courts interpreted contract and property laws and due process, they were not applying eternal verities but legislating their own social philosophy into law. Needless to say, this last did not earn him accolades either on Wall or State Street.

There was always a frenetic, even manic edge to him, with bursts of energy followed by periods of depression. Those who, like his second wife, Edith Kermit Carow, knew him best insisted that he was a far more complex person than the popular image indicated. Behind his seeming spontaneity there was often considerable calculation. At the same time, there was little that was cold-blooded and dissembling about him; he threw himself fully into whatever he did. His well-known saying, "black care rarely sits behind a rider whose pace is fast enough," is not without insight into what lay behind his pursuit of the Strenuous Life. To understand the nature of T. R.'s approach to public life, it seems essential to take the evidence of his early years into account.

The publication of his *Autobiography* in 1913 did much to deploy the Roosevelt "legend," both in what was said and what was omitted. The familiar story of the sickly child who by dint of sheer willpower cured himself of asthma, built up his physique, and transformed himself into a robust, vigorous he-man was only partly true. Not acknowledged in his narrative was the element of deliberate, self-conscious exhibition. He not only taught himself to be brave and bold, but he also strove mightily to *be seen* as brave and bold; he disguised the doubt and the hesitation, both from himself and from others. He also had a way of disregarding what did not fit into his story; he did not, for example, cure himself of asthma, but suffered from it intermittently throughout his life.

Much has been made, and rightly so, of T. R.'s attitude toward his father's hiring of a substitute to fight in the Union Army during the Civil War. Theodore Roosevelt, Senior, was otherwise his eldest son's hero; his decision not to serve in the army, despite his strong support of the Union cause, was based on the fact that his young wife, Martha Bulloch Roosevelt, was a native of Georgia, with two brothers who were prominent Confederate naval officers. Securing a substitute was by no means without precedent in well-to-do New York society, but after the war the elder Roosevelt apparently came to regret his decision.

What is obvious is that much of his son T. R.'s eagerness to demonstrate his own martial valor and ardor was a response to his father's failure to serve. When the war with Spain came in 1898, he resigned as assistant secretary of the Navy, recruited the regiment of Rough Riders, and earned high battlefield distinction in Cuba. In 1917, at age fifty-nine, overweight, and in poor health, he vainly sought permission to raise a division to fight in France, and he not only urged his four sons to volunteer but even brought his political influence to bear to get them overseas as soon as possible. Ted, Jr., and Archibald were severely wounded and Quentin, the youngest, died in aerial combat.

T. R.'s admiration for his father has been much attested. From all accounts the senior Roosevelt was an admirable figure, handsome, devoted to his family, with a strong sense of civic responsibility and an imposing record of public and charitable accomplishments. His death in 1878, at age forty-six, was devastating to T. R., who wrote in his diary that "I often feel badly that such a wonderful man as Father should have had a son of so little worth as I. I could not help reflecting sadly on how little use I am, or ever shall be in the world, *not through lack of perseverance and good intentions, but through sheer inability.* I realize more and more every day that I am as much inferior to Father morally and mentally as physically" (Dalton, *Theodore Roosevelt,* 69; the italics are mine).

Without questioning the sincerity of the young T. R.'s love and admiration for his father, one is a bit skeptical that the relationship was quite so simple as that. Diaries, it is true, are ostensibly written for the eye of the diarist alone—but they are intended for purposes of future reading, sometimes by others but certainly by the diarist himself. It is interesting that not only when writing the passage quoted above but for weeks and even months after his father's death, the young T. R. went to such lengths to record his continuing grief and reiterate his unworthiness. Especially considering the phrase that I have italicized, there is the sense that he was engaged both in lamenting the elder Roosevelt's loss and also in declining to accept ethical responsibility for his own failures.

After all, from everything we know of psychology, it would be odd if there were not some ambivalence to the emotional relationship of an adolescent son and his father, particularly this son. The filial admiration for the beloved parent and the grief at his loss are there and are genuine; but so, too, is an element of guilt—and this not only over his inability to live up to the example his father had set for him, but also at feeling insufficiently remorseful over the failure to do so. The italicized interjection appears to be a protest, and to suggest the presence, along with the grief, of resentment and anger—resentment at being made to feel unworthy, anger at having to suppress the resentment.

T. R. was never one to engage in excessive self-examination of his own motives. As Kathleen Dalton notes in her introduction, "Escape and flight from pain provided familiar devices to protect himself from his own strong emotions and from unpleasant facts he wanted to avoid" (5). The prolonged, repeatedly expressed lamentation in the diary is interesting, in that it is contrary to what soon became a conviction on his part that the way to master severe personal loss was to think about it as little as possible, and to avoid alluding to it. To do otherwise, he would later insist, was weak and morbid.

Such was his response five years afterward to the sudden, catastrophic deaths on February 14, 1884, of Alice Lee, his twenty-two-year-old first wife, after giving birth to a daughter, and ten hours later the same day, of Mittie, his mother, at age forty-eight. The distraught T. R. turned the infant, likewise named Alice, over to his older sister, Bamie, for raising, and not until after his marriage to Edith Carow did the child come to live with him, and then at Bamie's insistence. Even then, he could not bear to have her called Alice; she was Baby Lee or Sister.

T. R.'s mother, known as Mittie, was tiny, vivacious, warm-hearted and pleasure-loving, a gifted storyteller, a gracious hostess. She was also something of a neurasthenic. Kathleen Dalton suggests that T. R. came in later years to view her as self-indulgent, and comments that in his response to her death there was no equivalent to the protracted distress and grief expressed when his father died. She quotes Alice Roosevelt Longworth, T. R.'s and Alice Lee's daughter, as having "confirmed that he 'was not nearly so devoted to his mother as he was to his father'" (89). David McCullough, however, while conceding the neurasthenia, sees her even so as "an exceptional person in her own right," and responsible for some of her son's most attractive qualities, including his phenomenal energy (*Mornings on Horseback*, 69).

As between Dalton and McCullough, the former's is the more substantial work, but in this instance I think McCullough is nearer to the mark. The letters that the youthful T. R. wrote to Mittie indicate a very close, devoted relationship; "Darling motherling," he addresses her. Moreover, McCullough notes the immediate affinity that developed between Mittie and Alice Lee. He even quotes one of T. R.'s diary entries, referring to wintertime sleighing: "When my sweetest little wife can't go, I always take dear Mother. It is lovely to live as we are now" (239). (It should be added that Alice Roosevelt Longworth in her later years was by no means an objective source on the attitudes of the various females of the Roosevelt family toward T. R.)

I have gone into matters of family and filial psychology because they may help to explain T. R.'s performance both as twenty-sixth

president and during the ten years that followed. He was just over fifty years old in 1909 when he turned over the presidency to his chosen successor, William Howard Taft, and departed on an African safari. Four years before, in 1904, upon election to a full term in the White House in his own right, he had declared, too readily as some thought, that because he had already served all but six months of one term after McKinley's assassination, he would not seek reelection. His friends and supporters were astounded, and most believed that it was a severe blunder, both because it was entirely proper for him to have run for a second term of his own, and because by eliminating himself so early from the 1908 race he was weakening his own political leverage with Congress as president. He told William Jennings Bryan that he liked his job and was stepping down with regret, "for I have enjoyed every moment of this so-called arduous and exacting task" (*Letters of Archie Butt,* edited by Lawrence F. Abbott [1924], 7).

Once out of office and back from Africa, he grew increasingly unhappy at having to look on from the sidelines. "Get it out of your mind, Theodore, you will never be president of the United States again," Edith Carow Roosevelt told her husband in 1910, after hearing him speculating about future plans with his protégé Henry Stimson (Dalton, 369). Yet by 1912, having convinced himself that Taft had allowed the Old Guard to recapture control of the Republican Party, he decided to contest the nomination. Although obviously the favorite of the rank and file, he was denied it—whereupon he ran as a Progressive, thereby splitting the Republican vote and all but ensuring the election of Woodrow Wilson.

It is questionable whether Taft could have defeated Wilson even if T. R. had accepted the verdict of the Republican convention and declined to bolt the party, while had T. R. succeeded in gaining the Republican nomination he, and not Wilson, might well have been elected. If rather than running as a Progressive T. R. had possessed sufficient patience to hold off in 1912—he was, after all, younger than either Taft or Wilson—and to wait another four years, it seems likely that he, and not the colorless Charles Evans Hughes, would have been the 1916 Republican nominee. Had that happened, his own widespread popularity could well have overcome the very narrow margin by which Wilson won reelection. For T. R., however, so lengthy a strategic deferral of his political ambitions was a virtual impossibility.

As it was, the T. R.–Wilson duel of 1912 was the main contest. In John Milton Cooper, Jr.,'s words, "The most colorful politician since the Civil War squared off against the most articulate politician since the early days of the Republic" (*The Warrior and the Priest* [1983], 140). The difference between them was basically one of personality—which, however, given the two people involved was quite enough to make them intense rivals. The Democratic candidate won by a plurality, not a majority, of the electorate, with Taft finishing third behind Roosevelt.

In important respects the "Bull Moose" Progressive political agenda of 1912 did not vary substantially from that of Wilson and the Democrats. Certainly the impressive program of legislation enacted during Wilson's first term embodied no small portion of the Progressive Party's goals. In marshalling public opinion to cajole and coax recalcitrant senators and cautious congressmen, Wilson, the former college professor and university president, proved to be as skillful as T. R.

Both of them had started out conservatively and had moved toward more radical social views, T. R. perhaps even more so than Wilson. Both were idealists; both believed strongly in their own rectitude. Wilson was the more private and withdrawn; he did not thrive in political give-and-take, took little delight in chumminess, and had few close friends and confidants. He neither liked nor trusted the press, and resented the rapid-fire questioning of press conferences. Nor does he seem to have possessed the unflagging energy that characterized Roosevelt Major, as H. L. Mencken termed T. R. (Franklin Roosevelt was Roosevelt Minor).

Wilson is remembered most of all for his valiant and, it must be said, unnecessarily obstinate battle to secure American participation in a League of Nations. Two decades after his death, as the menace of a second world war grew and the nations of Western Europe seemed powerless to stand up to German aggression, he came to be viewed as a prophet. This is what we remember; in John M. Blum's words, "The apotheosis of Wilson depends on his devotion to the cause of continuous peace through world organization" (*Joe Tumulty and the Wilson Era* [1951], 169). In the post–World War II era, as it became apparent that the League's successor, the United Nations, would likewise be no guarantee of international peace and goodwill, Wilson's losing cause has come to seem less tragic and rather more ironic.

As for T. R., it is neither for ideas nor ideals that we continue to find him intriguing, so much as for his personality. The stands he took on specific issues—international cooperation, trust-busting, expansionism, conservation, labor, war, home and the family, or anything else—constitute parts of his sheer vitality. If the times were made to order for T. R., it can also be said that he set his own impress upon them. By no means the most unequivocal progressive of the Progressive Era, he was by all odds the most interesting. That so remarkable and many-sided a human being was in direct contact with just about everything that was important in American public life during his adult years has kept his memory alive.

T. R.'s last years were not his finest. From the 1912 election until his death in January 1919, he was very much a loose cannon on the gun-deck, as he himself put it, out of office and ever more resentful of Wilson for being in it. The outbreak of war in Europe in 1914 soon set him on a rampage. He raged against Wilson for not giving greater support to the Allies, then when war was declared in 1917 for his failure to prepare the nation for intervention, then as victory neared for being too lenient on Germany. Favorable at first to the idea of an international peacekeeping body once the war was won, he came to oppose it as a betrayal of American sovereignty. As Dalton says, toward the end his hatred of Wilson "may have been the passion that kept him going" (497).

There was a touch of megalomania to some of T. R.'s later utterances, as John Milton Cooper, Jr., remarks of T. R.'s famous comment about the forthcoming presidential race in 1916: "It would be a mistake to nominate me unless the country has in its mood something of the heroic—unless it feels not only devotion to ideals but the purpose measurably to realize those ideals in action" (*The Warrior and the Priest*, 304). Underlying all his censure of Woodrow Wilson's actions in 1917–1918, Cooper says, was "that one question—who in America could provide properly heroic leadership at this world-shaking time in history—who but himself? The cause of his quarrel with Wilson was Roosevelt's sublime egotism" (307).

That last may be carrying the argument a little too far; T. R., after all, was by no means the only leading Republican progressive who had scathing things to say on the subject. Certainly there was that about Wilson's personality and his way of doing things which encouraged extreme utterance on the part of his opponents. All the same, some of T. R.'s comments seem irresponsible, as in the press release he issued to America's allies and enemies in the wake of the striking Republican gains in the 1918 congressional election, and on the eve of Wilson's departure for the Peace Conference in Paris: "Mr. Wilson has no authority whatever to speak for the American people at this time. His leadership has just been emphatically repudiated by them" (Dalton, 511).

Granted, Wilson himself had sought to make that election into a referendum on his leadership, urging the voters to demonstrate their approval by electing Democratic candidates. Moreover, at the time T. R. was hospitalized and in pain, and, as it turned out, within weeks of his death. Even so, Wilson was the elected president of the United States, with two years still to serve. In any event, T. R. constituted no exception to John Blum's observation that "Never in American history has a national crisis been severe enough to overcome partisan politics" (*Joe Tumulty and the Wilson Era,* 146). He spoke out loudly and repeatedly for military preparedness, proclaiming Wilson and the Democratic administration as cowardly. The notion of "peace without victory" infuriated him. When the United States entered the war, he urged harsh treatment for pacifists and slackers, and tended to equate political disagreement with moral turpitude.

Measured, judicious response to opposing viewpoints was never T. R.'s style. Throughout his career he could and frequently did become irate over everything from "nature fakers"—writers who attributed sentimental motives to wildlife—to corporate "Malefactors of Great Wealth." The German torpedoing of the *Lusitania* in 1915 was the outcome of Wilson's "abject cowardice and weakness" (Cooper, *The Warrior and the Priest,* 303). Wilson was "the demagogue, adroit, tricky, false, without one drop of loftiness in him" (Owen Wister, *Roosevelt: The Story of a Friendship* [1930], 355). "As for shame, he has none," he wrote to Hiram Johnson, "and if anyone kicks him, he brushes his clothes, and utters some lofty sentence" (*The Warrior and the Priest,* 317).

Kathleen Dalton reports on Roosevelt's numerous rhetorical excesses. In his vehemence against pacifists and opponents of U.S. entry in the war, she points out, he provided aid and comfort to the advocates of intolerance and injustice that he otherwise denounced. He attacked the Wilson administration for attempting to censor criticism of its policies, yet he called Senator Robert La Follette of Wisconsin an "unhung traitor" for criticizing U.S. intervention in the war. He spoke out repeatedly against "hyphenated-Americanism" and the foreign-language (i.e., German-American) press, yet insisted that he was opposed to anti-immigrant nativism. In Cooper's words, "he was appealing to the despised opposite of his own convictions—to the isolationist, anti-interventionist, and parochial sentiments he had fought for over twenty years" (*The Warrior and the Priest,* 311).

Even so, during that period this high-born conservative Republican moved steadily in the direction of greater radicalism on domestic issues, anticipating much of the social legislation that his fifth cousin Franklin D. Roosevelt's New Deal would enact in the 1930s. Dalton chronicles at length his support for women's suffrage, denunciation of racial violence, and his advocacy of old-age and unemployment insurance, an excess profits tax, and graduated inheritance and income taxes.

She does her best to stress the firmness of those commitments—and there can be little doubt that T. R. believed what he was saying when he said it. Still, in his militant hostility to Wilson's goal of American commitment to participation in an international peacekeeping force for the League of Nations, T. R. was allying himself with the Republican Old Guard whose hegemony he had challenged as a Progressive. The public mood, both Republican and Democratic, was veering away from further reform and toward what the president who followed Wilson in 1921 would call "not nostrums but Normalcy." Had T. R. lived to run for president again in 1920, it seems quite possible that, master politician that he was, he would quickly have sensed an altered climate of opinion and adjusted his program accordingly. By this I do not mean that he would have retracted his more advanced social positions, so much as found other issues to emphasize.

Given T. R.'s temperament, it is difficult to imagine him as thriving during the Roaring Twenties. If his talents had been just right for the American political scene in the early 1900s, very likely the opposite would have been true in the moral letdown that followed the end of the war. So perhaps it is just as well that he was removed from the scene before the era of Harding and Coolidge got under way.

In the course of writing *Theodore Roosevelt: A Strenuous Life*, Kathleen Dalton would appear to have become so fond of her subject—and with T. R. that is hard not to do—that, while readily conceding his shortcomings, inconsistencies, and blind spots, she has been sometimes overly ready to accept his own version of what motivated those who opposed him. This is especially true with his archrival Woodrow Wilson, even though she does note that on important issues they were more often than not in agreement. Her explanation of why, for example, Wilson refused to allow Roosevelt to recruit and lead a volunteer division overseas in 1917 is one-sided and simplistic. After describing Roosevelt's interview with Wilson in April of 1917, she declares that "As he thought about the Roosevelt Division, Wilson had every reason to fear T. R. politically and therefore to prevent another San Juan Hill from electing T. R. president in 1920. So he turned T. R. down" (477).

The cause-and-effect of that last sentence is misleading. Undoubtedly the potential political ramifications were a factor in Wilson's decision, as indeed they must have been for T. R. as well. But Wilson and Secretary of War Newton Baker were convinced, too, that for so massive a military enterprise as would be needed against the German army on the Western Front, the catch-as-catch-can recruiting of the past would not do. The democratic way to proceed, Wilson and his military leadership believed, was through conscription: a selective service law administered by local civilian boards.

There were to be no appointments of politicians to high command this time, and no headlong rush of volunteers into uniform. Already the officers and potential officers needed to train and to lead into battle the troops who would make up the vastly enlarged American Army were in short supply, and a disproportionate number of T. R.'s proposed volunteers would fall into that category. There must be no pejorative distinctions between volunteers and draftees, and no priorities demanded for volunteer units, whether of equipment or in assignments.

As the newly appointed commander of the American Expeditionary Force, Major General John J. Pershing, wrote to explain why despite his own career obligations to T. R. he had opposed letting him raise a volunteer division. For the kind of warfare that lay ahead "it was necessary that officers, especially those in high command, be thoroughly trained and disciplined. Furthermore, he [T. R.] was not in the best of health and could not have withstood the hard work and exposure of the training camps and trenches" (*My Experiences in the World War* [1930], vol. 1, 22). In France, Pershing needed—and he used—the authority to replace division commanders on the spot during a battle or a campaign, and it is not difficult to imagine the furor that would have been touched off if it had proved necessary to relieve Roosevelt of command.

Woodrow Wilson could hardly have overridden the advice of not only his secretary of war but also the commanding general under whom T. R. would have served on the Western Front. And it must have been obvious to all concerned that, however T. R. might claim, and with entire sincerity, that bygones would be bygones and that if appointed he would be totally loyal to those in command over him, the chances were not very good of his staying silent for very long if he thought that mistakes were being made, in particular by Democrats.

So I disagree with Dalton. That said, I would insist that *Theodore Roosevelt: A Strenuous Life* is an interesting, well-written, and well-documented biography of a very complex and enduringly admirable man. He was no picture-book hero but, as Dalton declares, he had the capacity to learn and to change his views.

As noted earlier, T. R. was not one to bare his innermost thoughts, whether to others or to himself. Introspection was not one of his talents, and the maelstrom of activity that characterized his everyday routine was among other things a way of keeping boredom and melancholy at bay. After his retirement from the presidency, and especially after his unsuccessful campaign as a Progressive in 1912, that proved ever more difficult to do, while the frustration at having no role to play in the war exacerbated his feeling of futility.

It seems quite likely that, as some who knew him have said, the death of his youngest son, Quentin, in aerial combat in July of 1918, together with the severe wounding of Theodore, Jr., and Archie in infantry action, brought a heavy burden of guilt. Such awareness would have been heightened by an intermittent suspicion on his part that he had in effect used his sons to reinforce his own emotional needs. He knew that he had encouraged them as children to compete with each other to prove their fearlessness, that when war came they had felt it obligatory, as his sons, to demonstrate their masculinity, and that they were, and knew that they were, in effect his surrogates in battle. "To feel that one has inspired a boy to conduct that has resulted in his death," he wrote, "has a pretty serious side for his father" (Dalton, 504).

For the three boys who survived, to be the "sons of the lion," as they termed themselves, entailed lifelong problems of identity. Ted, Jr., had a distinguished career as a diplomat and in World War II as a battlefield soldier, earning the Congressional Medal of Honor for his leadership at Utah Beach on D-Day, yet from all accounts he experienced much unhappiness and was known for possessing an overweening ego. Dalton quotes Edith Roosevelt as having written to him in 1939 that "Honestly, as I look back, you fared worst because Father tried to 'toughen' you, but happily was too busy to exert the same pressure on the others" (516). Kermit ended as an alcoholic and a suicide. Archie grew bitter about his father, became a fanatical right-winger, and embarrassed the family with his extreme racist and political views.

If T. R.'s domestic political goals were in important respects similar to those of Woodrow Wilson, the twentieth-century public figure that he most resembled, it seems to me, was surely not Wilson, but rather Winston Churchill. The parallels are striking. Both were renowned for their furious activity, and apparently both were manic depressives. Both were aristocrats. Both had prominent fathers who died in their forties, and mothers who were sometimes self-indulgent. Both overcame childhood handicaps, in T. R.'s instance asthma and a weak physique, in Churchill's a speech defect and parental neglect. Both deliberately set out to cultivate robustness and to demonstrate their bravery under fire. Both attained early renown as war heroes. Both became well-known authors, but never at the expense of active involvement in politics. Both began as Tories, enlarged their sympathies as they matured, and made their reputations as reformers. Both encountered criticism as opportunists and party bolters. Both suffered severe setbacks in midcareer. Both spent time in the political wilderness, and found it greatly frustrating.

Where the similarity ends is in their later careers. There was for T. R. no equivalent to Churchill's reemergence in 1940 as Britain's great wartime leader. Had T. R. lived, and had he been a decade or two younger, something like that might well have happened; there can be no doubt about what his attitude would have been to Adolf Hitler and the rise of Nazism. It was left, however, to another, younger Roosevelt to deal with the challenges of crippling economic depression, the rise of totalitarianism, and a second and even more lethal world war, fought out on a more global scale and in close partnership with Churchill.

For Franklin Delano Roosevelt, who had married T. R.'s niece Eleanor, "Uncle Ted" was very much a role model. Both in politics and style F. D. R. deliberately evoked the Progressive heritage. "We stand at Armageddon, and we battle for the Lord!" went T. R.'s famous summons to the Progressives in 1912; "This is not a nomination; it is a call to arms!" F. D. R. declared in accepting the Democratic nomination in 1932.

The younger Roosevelt had gone through his own iron time in the 1920s, and been seasoned through it. He was longer on patience than T. R. had been, more in control of himself, and far more introspective and, it must be said, more devious. The problems of leadership facing F. D. R., first during economic depression and then in war, were more immediately urgent than those that either T. R. or Woodrow Wilson had confronted as president. He had learned from some of his older cousin's missteps, and also from watching T. R.'s great duel for power with Wilson, in whose administration he had been assistant secretary of the Navy. Not only were there old Progressives in F. D. R.'s cabinet from the outset of his administration, but when war drew near he acted to enlist as secretaries of the Navy and of war two prominent Republicans, one of them a Rough Rider in 1898, the other a political protégé of T. R.'s. He took care to keep the lines open to the Senate and House; there would not be for him the chasm between the White House and Congress that T. R. had allowed to develop during his second term, or that blighted Wilson's last several years as president.

What both the Roosevelts, Churchill, and for that matter Woodrow Wilson had in common was the ability to lead. They took full responsibility for the actions of the governments they headed, and those who worked with them were left in no doubt over who was making the major decisions. Sometimes this could have its disadvantages: F. D. R.'s obstinate refusal to accept Charles de Gaulle's growing authority in France; Churchill's insistence upon fighting the 1945 parliamentary elections along blatantly partisan lines; Wilson's converting the 1918 congressional election into a referendum on the Democratic Party's conduct of the war. In T. R.'s instance, his reluctance to consult with congressional leadership, especially during his second presidential term, ultimately placed him and his program at a virtual impasse with the House and Senate, but not before he had led the federal government decisively into the twentieth century. For all his reputation for spontaneity, on major policy decisions he thought things through in advance, was careful to prepare the way, and made it clear that he was calling the shots.

As the English ambassador, Lord Bryce, commented after T. R.'s last and most bitter clash with Congress, "Nobody likes him now but the people"(*Theodore Rex*, 547). From the death of William McKinley and T. R.'s elevation to the White House onward, for two decades there was probably not a presidential election that he could not have won, if allowed by the Republican establishment to head his party's ticket. As he prepared to leave the White House in 1909, Archie Butt, his naval aide, was convinced that "he better understands the American people than any one man in the past fifty years . . ." (*Letters of Archie Butt*, 357).

Several thousand Washingtonians, including numerous members of the diplomatic corps, showed up at the Union Station to say goodbye when the Roosevelt family left Washington following Taft's inauguration. Even Henry Adams, that acerbic, ironic old crosspatch who had mocked and made fun of him for years, went up to T. R. and Edith as they were leaving the White House and said, simply and meaningfully, "I shall miss you very much" (Owen Wister, *Roosevelt: The Story of a Friendship, 1880–1919* [1930], 149). And to a friend Adams wrote that his own house on Lafayette Square "will seem dull and sad when my Theodore has gone" (*Theodore Rex*, 520).

Among those at the station, and in tears, was Jules Jusserand, ambassador of the Republic of France, and T. R.'s tennis partner, fellow hiker, cliff-climber, and medieval scholar. As Jusserand once put it to

Archie Butt after coming for tea and listening to T. R. hold forth upon paleontology for more than two hours, "Was there ever such a man before?" (*Letters of Archie Butt*, 144).

There are even those who say that we could use someone like him at the helm right now.

8

Did Churchill "Ruin the Great Work of Time"?

Thoughts on the New British Revisionism

(1994)

> [Who] Could by industrious valor climb
> To ruin the great work of Time,
> And cast the kingdom old
> Into another mold. . . .
>
> —*Andrew Marvell, "An Horatian Ode upon*
> *Cromwell's Return from Ireland"*

Writers of history have always been good at second-guessing; in large measure it is their trade. These days the history of the Second World War is currently being rewritten by certain young British historians, who are eager to show that it was all a dreadful mistake, and the British should have stayed out and allowed the Germans and Russians to fight each other until exhausted, thereby preserving the Empire and keeping the Americans from taking over.

In such a thesis, the heroes are the sometime appeasers—Neville Chamberlain, Stanley Baldwin, Neville Henderson, Viscount Halifax, Sir Samuel Hoare, Sir John Simon, and the others who sought to placate Adolf Hitler and keep the Germans turned eastward in search of new countries to conquer. The villain, naturally enough, is Winston Churchill, whose great speech of defiance—"we shall fight on the landing grounds, we shall fight in the fields and in the streets, we shall fight in the hills, we shall never surrender. . . . "—was no more than "sublime nonsense." The verdict is John Charmley's, in *Churchill: The End of Glory*, the American edition of which was published late in 1993 by Harcourt Brace Jovanovich (411).

It was nonsense, the argument goes, because in June 1940, with French resistance crumbling and the victorious Wehrmacht setting up operations along the English Channel coast, the only way that Hitler could be stopped was by getting the United States involved. To do that, it would be necessary to mortgage all one's imperial wealth and possessions to the Americans, who would surely take advantage of the situation to become the dominant power, happily drain Britain of her resources, and leave her bereft of empire, prosperity, and *amour-propre*. To quote Charmley again, "It was certainly better to be an American rather than a German protectorate, but given that the war was being fought to preserve Britain's independence and a balance of power, that reflection was of little comfort to many Englishmen" (440).

Neville Chamberlain and the Conservative leadership realized that Britain couldn't afford to wage another world war, and that even if the war were won she would wind up in hock to the Yanks—who in Mr. Charmley's words "were, in fact, foreigners who disliked the British Empire even more than did Hitler" (430). So the Tory leaders did their best to conciliate the Führer, and when that failed and they were obliged to declare war, they planned to sit tight and do nothing that might cause trouble. But that didn't work, either, so when Hitler invaded and overran France and the Low Countries, they were prepared to face up to the facts of life and seek to arrange a peace agreement.

Alas, Winston Churchill wouldn't let them get away with it. Filled with romantic dreams of glory and sentimental nostalgia for the nineteenth century, the far-flung battle line, and dominion over palm and pine, he insisted that Britain was in the war to defeat Nazi Germany, and there was no alternative to military victory. Not only did he think it would be "certainly better to be an American rather than a German protectorate," but he was sufficiently deluded to believe that acquiescence in a Nazi-dominated Europe would be unthinkable, that no treaty with Hitler would be worth the paper it was printed on for very long, and that an England that might be permitted to carry on under Adolf Hitler's sufferance would be no England worth living in at all.

So, instead of seeking an agreement that would have enabled Britain to hold onto its cash reserves and keep its Empire intact, Churchill insisted on the expenditure of "blood, toil, tears and sweat" in order to "wage war, by sea, land and air, with all our might and with all the strength that God can give us" in pursuit of "Victory—victory at all costs" (401).

Thus misled, the British people stood up to Hitler long enough for the United States and the Soviet Union to join the fray, with the result that Nazi Germany was defeated. The price of national honor turned out to be financial bankruptcy, loss of the Empire, the end of British status as a world power, Soviet domination of Eastern Europe, and American leadership of the Free World—in short, the End of Glory.

So argues John Charmley, in a revisionist biography whose 649 pages of text and 52 pages of double-columned notes belie the fact that it is in inception and execution a partisan tract, with an animus against its subject that will grant him absolutely nothing. The Winston Churchill of this volume is an almost unmitigated disaster to his country. To find this book's counterpart one must turn to the debunking biographies of the 1920s, or Lytton Strachey on Cardinal Manning, or John T. Flynn on Franklin D. Roosevelt, or perhaps H. L. Mencken on Woodrow Wilson.

That Sir Winston was a flawed human, who made mistakes, that he was no stranger either to ambition or to egocentricity, has long been known. But that he recognized the evil of Nazi Germany almost at once when others did not, and led his island nation in a heroic fight to preserve its freedom, and in so doing—and in no merely metaphorical sense—saved the Western world, has been generally conceded.

What is happening now, however, is that as memories of those days and the emotions they evoked have ebbed, a new school of historians has come forth, whose members never knew the sound of air-raid sirens or the drone of buzz bombs, heard the Führer's voice over the wireless pledging vengeance upon England, or sang "There'll Always Be an England." What's so great about having saved the Western world from the Nazis? they want to know. Why wasn't Adolf Hitler allowed to go his own way unhindered, and the people of Continental Europe left to fend for themselves? What did the deaths of multimillions of European Jews, Slavs, and others matter in the scheme of things?

II

Revisionist history-writing is, of course, no new phenomenon. These days it is characteristic of the British right; in the 1960s and 1970s the revisionists were from the political left. What is common to all such activity is the intent to effect a violent reversal of the reigning historical consensus, whatever that may happen to be at the time. The young historians of the New Left in the 1960s and 1970s were busily proving that the Cold War was a conspiracy of American imperialism, and the Marshall Plan no more than a scheme for the economic victimization of the Third World. The motive for all this was obvious: it was a way of protesting against the war in Vietnam. What better way to do that, if one were a historian, than to demonstrate that one's elders were self-serving hypocrites, who used pious platitudes to cloak cynical aggressiveness and economic buccaneering?

To say this is not to contend that there is no place for revised interpretation of the past, or that the reasons why people say and believe that they have acted at various junctures in history are necessarily sacred. Unexamined assumptions, half-truths, fallible judgments, and special pleadings have ever been the way of humankind. At the same time, though, if there is one thing that may be learned from the study of historiography, it is that the needs and the values of the historian's own time play an important part in the interpretation of the past. Nor must one be a historical relativist to acknowledge the difficulties of any attempt to put oneself in the place of the historical figures of a different era, and to see the world and their place within it as they viewed such things. Human nature itself may not change very much, but the terms whereby that nature expresses itself can differ profoundly from one era to another.

The revisionist impulse, however, involves more than merely an impulse to interpret the past anew. There is, after all, a considerable difference between recognizing that the assumptions of a historian's own day are bound to color any assessment of the past, and setting out to write history with the fervent conviction that all previous efforts to interpret the subject one is scrutinizing were no more than willful distortions of truth, compounded of mythology and self-congratulation, and therefore crying out for unmasking.

What propels the dedicated revisionist is the urgent desire to upset the applecart, and to play the role of fearless exposer of the previous generation's historical evasions, clever distortions, and crafty cover-ups. Add to this a measure of *épater le bourgeois,* and you have not only John Charmley and today's young Brits but also the writing of history as a species of parricide.

III

The current World War II revisionism is emanating principally from political conservatives—Charmley describes himself as a right-wing Thatcherite. No breathtaking imaginative leap is needed to recognize why this might be so. Great Britain is not only no longer a major political and military power, but in industrial and economic position it has receded to the second rank. The British Empire, the dissolution of which Churchill announced he had no intention of presiding over, is not of transcendent importance in the global scheme of things.

Meanwhile the Cold War that followed the destruction of the Axis Powers in World War II has ended; the Berlin Wall and the Iron Curtain have been dismantled, and East and West Germany have resumed existence as a single nation. In effect the economic and cultural malaise that surfaced in the late nineteenth century, reached crisis proportions in 1914, and thereafter for some eight decades divided the Western world into opposing armed camps, has finally resolved itself. This is not to say, of course, that there will not be new crises, but these are likely to be of a different sort and draw upon different alignments of forces.

Over the course of that eighty-year period there were various switches in national allegiance, but the one abiding tie throughout the entire time was that between Great Britain and the United States. However tardy the U.S. may have been in entering both wars, and despite momentary divergences such as the Suez affair in 1956, there has been a continuity in cultural, social, and, in the last analysis, political outlook that has been as deep-seated as it has been pervasive. Its existence was demonstrated again during the Falkland Islands episode of 1982.

What has happened, however, is that Great Britain's status within what Churchill called "the English-speaking peoples" has changed from one of senior partner, to coequal, and then to subordinate. At the close of the first decade of the twentieth century, the British Empire seemed to be at its grandest—an island kingdom of some 38 million people exercising economic and political suzereignty over an empire of some 350 million constituting a quarter of the world's population. But the head start in industrialization and the political stability that had enabled Britain to establish and maintain its empire had ceased to provide the necessary competitive edge. Not only were other empires being carved out, but the natives were getting increasingly restless.

At least from the days of the Boer War onward, the evidence that the Empire was in trouble was there to read. The transformation in relative importance was taking shape throughout the period 1880–1914; the First World War made it obvious; the Second World War confirmed it; and the decades of the Cold War completed the process. Colonial empires have not coped very well over the past half century, and without the wealth of a colonial empire to sustain it, the United Kingdom was unable to retain its position. Militarily, economically, and to a certain extent culturally—though, and this is important, *not* for the high culture—the United States has become by far the more powerful partner.

IV

To appreciate the effect of the above upon certain young Englishmen of right-wing persuasion, it is important to keep in mind that this shrinkage of wealth and power took place at the same time that the British ruling class was losing its hegemony over government and finance. Although undeniably facets of the class system still remain, the period from the First World War onward has seen a formidable democratization of British life. As David Cannadine demonstrates in *The Decline and Fall of the British Aristocracy* (1990), the old British Establishment's control was far more massive than that in any other European nation, and its erosion thus all the more traumatic. "Between 1880 and 1914, the world that [young British patricians] had been brought up to dominate and to control had emphatically turned against them. And between 1914 and 1918, it was turned completely upside-down" (37).

World War II and the Labour government put the finishing touches on the transaction. To quote Cannadine, "In the world of Wilson and Callaghan, Heath and Foot, public life in Britain was less aristocratic than it had been in the days of Attlee. And in the rampantly petty-bourgeois world of Thatcher, where self-made men are her ideal, the old territorial class appears—with very few exceptions—at best anachronistic and at worst plain irrelevant" (638).

What all this meant was that wealth, education, and family connections no longer provided automatic entrée and status, whether for a young gentleman or, as often happens, a young scion of the middle class equipped with a university education and covetous of rising to privileged station. Indeed, for the latter it is likely to be an especially dismaying business. To have worked so hard to attain elevation to the Establishment, and then to find that it no longer runs the show! It is like sneaking under what looked like a circus tent, only to find that a revival is going on inside.

Is it any wonder, then, that a young academic historian of Tory sentiments and loyalties, entering upon a career at a time when the Cold War drew to an end and a realization of the diminished status of Britain seemed to coincide with the greatly reduced status of the old Establishment, might look around for a target, a scapegoat upon which to heap all one's resentment of the lowered expectations and worsened estate? And that, having no personal memories of what Churchill called his countrymen's "finest hour" and reviewing what happened from a perspective dominated by dissatisfaction at the diminished present, he would find precisely that target in the person of the statesman who led his country at the time of greatest peril, and who did indeed, however unwillingly, "preside over the dissolution of the British Empire"? That in fact it had been going on at an accelerating pace for more than half a century before Churchill became prime minister was irrelevant. Churchill was in place when the mortgage came due; therefore he was to blame for borrowing the money.

It is this frame of mind that accounts for the emotional fervor which seems to be producing not only John Charmley's indictment of Churchill and his earlier apologia for Neville Chamberlain and his umbrella diplomacy, but also a spate of revisionist works of history calling into question the values and assumptions on which the conduct of British affairs was based during the greater part of the twentieth century.

Not surprisingly, there has been an attempt to refurbish the tarnished reputations of those historical figures such as Chamberlain and Lord Halifax who, whether by intention or general debility of spirit, sought to delay or to avoid coming to grips with the menace of Nazi Germany. Andrew Roberts's biography of Halifax, *The Holy Fox* (1991), for example, depicts that sad-eyed temporizing Tory as a much-maligned statesman: "it was largely due to his unceasing efforts for peace that Britain could enter the war as the champion of wronged and outraged Civilization" (308).

It was also due to Halifax and his associates that every effort to stop Hitler before he could play havoc with that civilization was thwarted, and that anyone who desired to do so was resolutely kept out of office. It was Halifax who visited the Third Reich in 1936 and made it quite clear to Hitler himself that Great Britain would have no objections to the Anschluss of Austria, the dismemberment of Czechoslovakia, and the enforced annexation of Danzig. Some "champion of wronged and outraged Civilization"!

There has also been an effort to rehabilitate Hitler's Germany itself, to suggest that, while of course its excesses are to be deplored, it was not really as monstrous as depicted, and after all, it was dedicated to defeating communism. (Either that, or the revisionist simply glides over the matter. Charmley, for example, can publish a biography of Churchill running to more than three hundred thousand words without having anything to say about Dachau, Auschwitz, Treblinka, etc.) By refusing to seek an accommodation with Hitler, Churchill and Franklin D. Roosevelt only made things worse for the Jews, Poles, and other victims of Nazi conquest. Besides, if left alone

Hitler would have concentrated his aggressive impulses on the *Untermenschen* of Eastern Europe. After all, the Führer really admired the English. Didn't he say so himself on several occasions?

And so on. I recently read a book by yet another young British historian which advanced the thesis that it was really France, and not Imperial Germany and Austria-Hungary, that was most to blame for causing the First World War! If one is going to revise history in order to find a culprit for the decline of the British Empire, why stop with Winston Churchill alone? Why not go back and rewrite the events leading up to 1914?

V

The nub of the revisionist argument is that if Britain had made peace with Hitler, whether before or after the Battle of Britain, the British Empire would have remained intact and the post-1945 Communist domination of Eastern Europe and the Cold War would not have happened. What can one say to such hindsight? The idea that in order to be able to concentrate Germany's full resources on his true heart's desire, the destruction of Soviet Russia, Adolf Hitler sincerely wanted peace, is undoubtedly correct provided that what is meant by "peace" is understood. Given Hitler's temperament and ambitions, "peace" on such terms would have consisted of a period of a few years during which the Wehrmacht thoroughly crushed the Soviet Union, paused to recuperate, and then proceeded to take care of the British. Indeed, Hitler himself said as much; at a conference with his generals on July 31, 1940, the Nazi dictator, as Matthew Cooper writes in *The German Army, 1933–1945* (1978), told them that "decisive victory could be achieved only by the defeat of Britain, but this might be brought about by elimination of the Soviet Union, which, together with the neutralization of the United States by the power of Japan, would end all hope" for the little island (255).

What the approach omits, for one thing, is the nature of the war lord that Hitler aspired to be and was. The notion that such a person, having crushed Russia and made himself master of the continent of Europe and much of Asia, would have been sated, and willing thereafter to coexist peaceably with Great Britain, flies in the face of several thousand years of recorded behavior on the part of military conquerors. When one victory is achieved and one nation subdued, the war lord looks around for another target. Each specified objective is at bottom no more than a means to permit a war to be waged. Why, for example, did Bonaparte choose to renew hostilities against England within two years after signing the Treaty of Amiens in 1802? He had achieved all his supposed objectives, extended the boundaries of France beyond those of the *ancien régime*, regained the overseas colonies seized by the British, secured the recognition of the crowned houses of Europe. There was no real economic or political logic to Napoleon's decision to recommence war. The warfare itself, the winning of victories on battlefields, was what he coveted.

In the same way, in order to unleash his armies Adolf Hitler invented the pretexts for his wars. As the Führer himself put it in 1943, "I am no ordinary soldier-king but a war lord—probably the most successful in history." If there is any hard evidence that he intended to stop finding pretexts to permit military onslaughts, no one has ever produced it. (As for what he would have done with the atomic bomb, on which his scientists were at work in the early 1940s, one shudders to think.)

The belief that because Hitler was bent upon attacking the Soviet Union, he should have been left to do so, and that the Nazi and Communist regimes would then have proceeded to exhaust each other's military might in a protracted war fought in Eastern Europe, is of course cherished by revisionists. It is an example of wishful looking back at its most glittering. (I should note here that John Charmley does not himself advance this particular argument itself. One gets the idea, however, from what he has to say about the Russians later on, that he would certainly not quarrel with the notion.)

Historically it presupposes that Great Britain could be certain that a German assault on the Soviet Union would turn into a knockdown, drag-out affair that would be exhausting to conqueror and conquered alike. But in 1940 and 1941 that was scarcely a permissible assumption. What with the overwhelming success of the Nazi blitzkrieg in Poland in 1939 and in Norway, France, and the Low Countries in 1940, as contrasted with the abysmal performance of the Red Army against Finland in 1939–1940, the probability of a rapid German conquest of the Soviet Union, at relatively little cost in manpower and equipment, was quite high. That Churchill and his military advisers could have foreseen the massive resistance that Russia was able to put up, and the ensuing three-and-a-half-year bloodletting, is most unlikely.

"Barbarossa," the German onslaught against Russia, was three-pronged: a northern thrust aimed at Leningrad, a central thrust through White Russia against Minsk, Smolensk, and ultimately Moscow, and a southern thrust through the Ukraine toward the Crimea and the Caucasus. Hitler's generals urged him to give primacy to the drive on Moscow, rather than to throw badly needed divisions and equipment into the drive southward. They reasoned that to capture Moscow would not only give them possession of the Soviet Union's political, economic, and military center and the heavy industrial facilities around and to the east of the capital, but also by destroying the center of the Russian communications system bring about a virtual paralysis of the enemy's ability to resist effectively. Hitler, however, refused to give priority to the capture of Moscow until too late in the summer, and then was unwilling to divert forces from the southern front to augment the attack. Even so, German spearheads eventually reached within ten miles of Moscow.

Had the Wehrmacht been able to use in the Barbarossa offensive even as many as half of the fifty-one divisions and equipment then deployed in Western Europe, and had the Luftwaffe been freed from the need to defend against British air attacks on the cities of Germany, it is quite likely that there would have been ample forces to take Moscow and to drive on to eliminate much of the heavy industry located beyond it. As Cooper points out in *The German Army, 1933–1945*, "If the advancing armies could achieve the line Leningrad-Moscow-Rostov before the winter [of 1941–1942] made further movement impossible, before the divisions from the Far East could move west, and before the Soviet mobilization machinery could produce too many field divisions, victory would indeed be possible."

So the fact that when Hitler invaded the Soviet Union, the British, though without a bridgehead on the continent, were still very much in the war and tying down almost one-fourth of the Wehrmacht's divisions and no small portion of the German air force clearly had a formidable impact upon the German failure to destroy the Soviet Union's powers of resistance in the swift, lethal campaign that Barbarossa was meant to be. Thus the hypothesis that Great Britain could have made peace and then allowed the German and Soviet war machines to wear each other out in Eastern Europe will not stand up to scrutiny.

VI

If . . . It is so tempting to isolate a single factor, a single action not taken or decision not made, without regard to its full historical context, and to say that if only this or that had been done, all would have turned out differently. The assumption is that whatever else happened afterwards would have stayed in place unchanged. But history doesn't work that way. One action causes a compensating action, which in turn results in another, and so on.

Even if it is assumed that Hitler would have been willing to allow Great Britain to go its own way once the Soviet Union had been conquered and subdued, which is a very great deal to assume, is it likely that a humiliated and demoralized United Kingdom could have held onto its overseas possessions for very long? What would have been the response of Canada to England's knuckling under? Would it have remained a loyal part of the British Empire? What would have happened when the Japanese moved upon the British territories and possessions in southeast Asia? And what of India? Would it have been content to stay quiescent?

How long would the Suez Canal, that vital link between the United Kingdom and its overseas possessions, have stayed under British control? Britain was also engaged in a war with Benito Mussolini's Fascist Italy. It is true that the Italian army had shown little aptitude for desert warfare in North Africa, and Germany had been forced to send an Afrika Korps to its rescue. But that Hitler would have stood by for very long once the Duce renewed his designs upon the British protectorates in North Africa and the Middle East seems improbable.

Moreover, the Spain of Francisco Franco, emboldened by Britain's acquiescence and with Hitler's encouragement and blessing, would surely have demanded the cession of Gibraltar. How long, therefore, would the Mediterranean Sea have remained open to the British navy and to British commerce? And how long would it have been before the industrial might of a victorious Germany, able now to draw upon the full resources of a conquered Europe, created a Luft-waffe of overpowering strength and a submarine fleet that could erase British shipping from the high seas?

What then of the great Empire that a peace agreement with Adolf Hitler supposedly would have been saved for Britain? Every likeli-hood is that it would have commenced to disintegrate almost at once, and the more so because, peace agreement or no peace agree-ment, Britain could not have dared to employ its fleet and its re-sources elsewhere in the face of even the possibility of a cross-channel invasion by the Germans.

Lastly, what would have been the impact, politically and psycho-logically, of such a pact with Nazi Germany upon Great Britain it-self? What would have been its effect upon the tradition of free speech, individual liberties, religious freedom, minority rights, and democratic government that, for all the lingering class system that still marked English society, had evolved over the course of five hun-dred years of immunity from foreign invasion? Would England have remained the England that we knew, and that we know today?

To put the question another way, could the England that we knew, the England of Winston Churchill, ever have consented, once en-gaged in a war, to accept a peace treaty dictated by Nazi Germany? To contend that it ought to have done so, that it was in its long-range economic interests to have done so, is, finally, irrelevant.

Churchill had come to power, after his long years of political ban-ishment, precisely because he embodied the national determination to stand up to the threat that Hitler's Germany constituted to British freedom. The evasions, moral compromises, and submissions of the 1930s were over. To suggest that the people of England—as distin-guished, perhaps, from the old men of the Conservative Party—would have been willing to acquiesce in what would obviously be a humiliating, craven settlement while that menace still existed, is to misread the times, the place, and the people.

In his biographical put-down of Britain's wartime leader, Charm-ley spends considerable effort in developing the point that in 1945 Churchill ended up acquiescing in Russian control of Poland, which he depicts as making a hypocrisy and travesty of Churchill's insis-tence upon combating Germany for attacking Poland in 1939—the implication being that in not wishing to stop Hitler, the appeasers were justified. As if there were no distinction to be made between a response to the naked and unprovoked aggression of Nazi Germany, and to the actions, however ruthless, taken to create a postwar defensive buffer of satellite states by a wartime ally whose borders had been invaded, cities devastated, and twenty million of whose citizenry had perished!

The creation of the Iron Curtain in 1945–1947, for all its potentiality for flare-ups, was basically a defensive measure. The Soviet Union's essential strategy in the ensuing Cold War was to move in where it could, but to stop short of war. It could be, and was finally, "contained." Hitler's Germany, by contrast, had only one posture: military conquest, and no strategy of containment could have worked for very long.

I noted earlier that Charmley is able to equate Hitler's domination of Europe during World War II with America's postwar economic and political hegemony. While to be subjected to the latter is "certainly preferable," the difference between the two is supposedly one of degree rather than of kind. With equal logic, one might say that having a wisdom tooth removed is "certainly preferable" to castration.

VII

It is Charmley's contention that the great error of Winston Churchill's thinking was his sentimental reliance upon the United States of America and its president, Franklin D. Roosevelt. In so arguing, he offers a picture of the American scene during the early years of the war that is difficult for one who actually remembers the period to recognize. I quote a representative comment: "Despite the Churchillian legend, to which American participants in the war were only too happy to pay lip-service later, there was no widespread desire in June or July 1940 to help the British" (429).

To students of twentieth-century American history, this will come as a considerable surprise. Certainly there was an articulate Isolationist contingent in the nation, particularly in the Midwest, and there would have been little support for entering the war as a belligerent at the time. But public opinion was overwhelmingly on the side of Britain; an opinion poll taken in July 1940 indicated that seven out of ten Americans believed that a Nazi victory would place the United States in danger, and so were in favor of assistance to the embattled British. Despite the parlous condition of American arms, the War Department turned over extensive stocks of surplus or outdated arms, munitions, and aircraft to Britain. In the month of June alone, more than $43 million worth of supplies were dispatched across the Atlantic. It wasn't much, but it was all the United States had; as late as a year later, America's own expanding armed forces were conducting maneuvers with make-believe weapons because the available equipment had been sent to England the summer before. Charmley to the contrary notwithstanding, the retrospective judgment of an operative in the German Abwehr military counter-intelligence service, that in the year 1940, America saved England is, though overstated, a more accurate summation of what the president and a large majority of the American people desired.

The United States, after all, was *not* at war with Germany in 1940, and Roosevelt was being savagely assailed by his opponents as a warmonger who if reelected would surely plunge the nation into war. The power to declare war was vested in Congress, not the president. What Roosevelt was able and willing to do under the circumstances seems, in retrospect, quite remarkable. If there were times when even a desperate Winston Churchill expressed exasperation at the seeming tardiness of the American response to what he perceived as the common danger, most reputable historians of the period would rate Roosevelt's efforts to support an embattled Britain as highly effective.

The fact that Americans in general, including Roosevelt, had no great admiration for Great Britain's far-flung Empire as such is another matter; when it came down to the question of England versus Nazi Germany, there was little doubt of where U.S. sympathies lay. Otherwise Roosevelt would not have been able to do what he did.

Without question the United States profited from the sale of arms, aircraft, munitions, and other material of war to Britain, and just as in World War I, it emerged from the conflict in far better economic condition than did its allies. The effect of England's involvement in the two wars was to bring it close to bankruptcy. The task of standing up to the enemies of the free world is an expensive business, as the United States subsequently discovered during the Cold War.

Moreover, like the United States, Britain now confronts the ironic fact that the two countries that were the principal enemies, Germany and Japan, have emerged from the long ordeal in highly prosperous condition, having been spared the expense of maintaining the military deterrent to Soviet expansion. This is very much a part of the dissatisfaction prompting the revisionist impulse, and understandably so. (I've no doubt that as the memory of the Berlin Airlift and the Korean War fades, the revisionists of a future era will be demonstrating that the defense of the West and the containment of the Soviet Union were quite unnecessary, and the North Atlantic Treaty Organization a waste of time and money. Indeed, the partisans of the New Left, in their zeal to attack our Vietnam involvement, were already saying as much in the late 1960s and 1970s.)

There is no point in taking up all of John Charmley's arguments in deflation of what he considers the "Churchill Myth." The basic thrust of the biography is that Churchill was a romantic Victorian whose egocentricity was exceeded only by his ambition. He is granted precious few statesmanly virtues. Even the notion that the reason why Churchill wanted, in 1943 and 1944, to carry the war into the Balkans was to prevent the advancing Russians from dominating all of Eastern and Central Europe is scouted. If Charmley is to be believed, Churchill had no such foresight, for he almost never took the long-range view of anything. His decisions were based on love of adventure and military audacity, not on rational calculation. The wartime prime minister comes off as a cross between Harry Hotspur and Don Quixote.

That the world, and in particular the Western world, would have been a more comfortable place to live in if it had managed to remain at peace can scarcely be doubted. The cost exacted by the failure of human beings to be wiser and more peaceable than they proved to be—close to one hundred million dead, untold billions of dollars spent on the materiel for killing them—is appalling to contemplate. Yet to single out a particular event during that time, a specific decision, and to say that if only it hadn't happened, or had happened differently, then all or most of the catastrophe could have been avoided, is a profitless undertaking. And to contend that individuals of goodwill, finding themselves caught up in that terrible happening, could or should have declined to stand up to both the immediate and the long-range threat posed to themselves, their countries, and all that they believed in, is to acquiesce in the very barbarity and destructiveness itself. It was indeed a time when, in the poet Yeats's words, "The best lack all conviction, while the worst / Are full of passionate intensity." Fortunately there was a Winston Churchill who saw what was at stake.

It is so tempting to look back at the eight decades of hot and cold war, and to try to argue that the whole wretched business was not worth the effort. But in essence what the argument amounts to is a fond wish that the twentieth century hadn't happened, that not only the war against Hitler's Germany but that against the Kaiser's Germany as well had never taken place, and that somewhere around the globe, for twenty-four hours of each day the sun still shone upon the Union Jack. Ernest Hemingway's character Jake Barnes provides the proper answer for this at the conclusion of *The Sun Also Rises*: "Isn't it pretty to think so?"

If one is a young Briton of relatively limited expectations who feels deprived of proper status and forced to make one's way in a plebeian world, it must indeed be pretty to think that it could and should all have happened differently, that by rights the Empire should still be intact, with Britannia continuing to rule the waves and the pre-1914 Establishment still in control of government. But it didn't happen that way, and scolding one's elders for standing up to Nazi Germany in 1940 will not bring back either the Empire or the Garden of Eden.

9

Ladies of the English Establishment
The Mitford Sisters and Violet Bonham Carter

(2003)

Let us begin with a brief look at the embattled British foxhunting situation, not for its own sake so much as for what it signifies. The House of Commons, with its Labour Party majority, has voted to ban the hunting of foxes with dogs, on the grounds that it constitutes cruelty to animals. The House of Lords has declined to go along. A constitutional crisis threatens, reminiscent of the great confrontation of nearly a century ago.

In 1908–1911 the Lords were made up to a large extent of members who held their seats by right of family inheritance, and, not surprisingly, a majority were Tories. The elected Liberal Party majority in the Commons enacted a budget which the Lords promptly vetoed. Three general elections and the threat of getting the King to appoint several hundred new Liberal peers were needed to force the Lords to give way, after which legislation was passed severely restricting the power of the Lords to block measures passed by the Commons.

Nowadays the House of Lords consists largely of appointed, not inheriting, peers, but these too tend to vote Conservative. As noted, they refused to ratify the ban on foxhunting. In response, the Labour Party in the Commons, which with some exceptions wishes the sport outlawed, threatens additional curbs on what the Lords can and cannot do. "There is no middle way," one Labour MP declares. "You can't compromise on cruelty." To which an organization known as the Countryside-Alliance promises to send five hundred thousand pro-foxhunters marching upon London. "The message must go out the length and breadth of this land—," a Conservative MP says; "we must fight for our country traditions and values."

What the foes of foxhunting object to is the fact that, while the scarlet-and-black-clad horsemen and horsewomen are galloping along happily and calling out "View Halloo!" the hounds run the fox to ground, corner it, and proceed to tear it to pieces. That, say the antis, constitutes inexcusable cruelty. The pro-hunting forces insist that pursuing foxes by hound and horn at break of day is essential to the time-honored traditions of rural Britain. (There are still 184 established hunts in England alone.)

So much for foxhunting per se. The underlying question, given the foxhunt's role as emblem of upper-class England, is whether its imperiled status, and the seeming helplessness of the House of Lords to protect it from the Commons, signifies that the old landed gentry can no longer, in any meaningful sense, be said to matter. If unable to safeguard the spectacle that a less-than-sympathetic Oscar Wilde once termed "the unspeakable in full pursuit of the uneatable," of what use is an Establishment to anyone?

On the other hand, the ferocity of the current dispute can also be interpreted as indicating that although much has been taken, much abides—and that an underlying allegiance to the principle of pedigree remains alive in the hearts of trueborn Britons.

In the 1950s Nancy Mitford, of whom more later, enthralled her fellow countrymen with an article that told them how to distinguish between "U" (for upper class) and "non-U" Britons by their choice of vocabulary: "looking glass" vs. "mirror," "sofa" vs. "settee," "lavatory paper" vs. "toilet paper," and so on. Supposedly it was intended largely as a spoof, but its widespread popularity indicated that an awareness of rank and station remained very much a part of the English consciousness. Subsequently, when one of her early novels was republished, Nancy told Evelyn Waugh that she had to rewrite much of it to bring it into conformity. (Nancy's sister Diana, wife of the British Fascist leader Oswald Mosley, also of whom more later, thought the article "vulgar.")

If so, does anyone care about such things? It seems that a lot of people still do. David Cannadine, who has chronicled the decline of the landed aristocracy, insists that a rooted belief in hierarchy still survives: "Britain retains intact an elaborate, formal system of rank and precedence, culminating in the monarchy itself, which means that prestige and honor can be transmitted and inherited across the generations" (*The Rise and Fall of Class in Britain* [1999], 22). Unlike Americans, Cannadine says, Britons automatically think of themselves in terms of hierarchy. There are essentially three ways of approaching matters of rank and caste, he notes: as elaborate hierarchy, with its various gradations; as tripartite—upper, middle, and lower; and as upper and lower—either/or, "them and us." Each of these methods has its proponents, and when interpreting the pronouncements of politicians, Cannadine says, it is important to determine which version is being used.

He has developed his subject in a half-dozen books, of which perhaps the best is *The Decline and Fall of the British Aristocracy* (1990)—though all are informative and well-written. Not one to let theory interfere with accurate observation, Cannadine proposes no dialectical argument, Marxist or otherwise, to account for the waning of the British upper-class Establishment—a waning that he favors. At the same time, he is not convinced that a majority of his fellow countrymen really desire to be rid of that particular incubus. He deplores the reverence still being paid to the cult of the Stately Homes of England in which the landed aristocracy once held forth, foxhunts and all: "Enough of snobbery and nostalgia. Good riddance to ignorance and sentimental deference. It is time we got beyond the country house" ("Beyond the Country House," *Aspects of Aristocracy* [1994], 245).

I offer no dissent from his conclusions, which seem sound enough. Cannadine is not only an impressive interpreter of the social history of the British Isles, but a deft stylist as well. His way of going about his business reminds me of the late C. Vann Woodward's method: striking assertion, followed by convincing illustrative incidences, the whole succinctly phrased. I would note only that there are times when his enthusiasm leads him to overstate his case. How, for example, could the near-scoundrel described in "Winston Churchill as Aristocratic Adventurer" (*Aspects of Aristocracy*) ever have transformed himself in to what at the very close of his essay Cannadine concedes he became in his finest hour?

Cannadine doesn't think very highly of the Harold Nicolsons, an estimate that I must say I share. Consider, however, the essay about them entitled "Portrait of More Than a Marriage," the opening sentence of which reads as follows: "Harold Nicolson and Vida Sackville-West were two very remarkable people; but that is no reason for regarding them as having been more remarkable than they actually were" (*Aspects of Aristocracy*, 210). The essay concludes nine thousand words later with the identical caveat, identically phrased. The reader might be led to wonder just how remarkable is very remarkable. In both these essays, and occasionally elsewhere, one has the sense that in his zeal to demonstrate the iniquities of inherited privilege, the author is not above doing a little cavilling.

In what follows, and with no further attention to the foxhunt crisis as such, I want to consider several books about the lives and times of certain prominent female members of the British upper-class Establishment during the just-completed twentieth century. In a general way, it seems to me, the first of these volumes (Mary S. Lovell, *The Sisters: The Saga of the Mitford Family* [2002]), exemplifies Cannadine's thesis. The six Mitford sisters were bona fide products of the landed aristocracy in an era when its function and inherited powers were rapidly dwindling. What was missing for them was a valid role in an altered time and place, and what they did and tried to do with their lives can be viewed as efforts to discover a suitable replacement for what had been lost.

Of Mitford girls there were six in all, along with a brother, Tom, who late in World War II was killed in Burma, where he was serving against the Japanese because he couldn't stomach the thought of fighting the Germans. Four of the girls achieved great notoriety. As their mother once remarked, "Whenever I see a headline beginning with 'Peer's Daughter' I know one of you children has been in trouble" (Lovell, 258). The sisters were, in order of appearance:

(1) Nancy, the novelist (*The Pursuit of Love, Love in a Cold Climate*, etc.), who was born in 1904; after 1945 she lived in Paris, where she was in love with one of Charles DeGaulle's top lieutenants, who had no intention of marrying her.

(2) Pamela (Pam), born in 1907, who was married to a scientist and Royal Air Force war hero, and was later divorced. Much of her later life was spent traveling; together with Debo (see below), Pam was the least off-beat of the crowd.

(3) Diana, born 1909, who married a wealthy Guinness heir, left him for Sir Oswald Mosley, politician, philanderer, ideologue, and head of the British blackshirts in the 1930s. During World War II the two spent three and a half years in prison. Diana wrote an autobiography, essentially a defense of Mosley's good intentions; also, a biography of Wallis Warfield Simpson and a family memoir.

(4) Unity Valkyrie (Bobo), born 1914, who had a crush on Adolf Hitler, moved to Berlin, spent much time in his company, was a friend of Joseph Goebbels and Julius Streicher, was ostentatiously pro-Nazi and anti-Semitic, and when war broke out in 1939 shot herself.

(5) Jessica (Decca), born 1917, who ran off to Spain at age nineteen with a wild young leftist cousin, then found a job with the U.S. government in Washington. Her husband joined the Royal Canadian Air Force, was lost and presumed drowned. She became an American citizen, married a young Jewish lawyer, joined the Communist Party, and later wrote several best-sellers.

(6) Deborah (Debo), who was the youngest, born in 1920, and married a young man who upon his elder brother's death in the war became the future Duke of Devonshire; in 1991 they celebrated their golden wedding anniversary. She wrote two books centered on their ducal estate, which she and her husband turned into one of the more widely visited Stately Homes of England, with a profitable mail-order catalog business.

So the tally is one Nazi, one Fascist, one Communist, and one novelist. Also, one traveler, and one duchess-entrepreneur. In all, six marriages, three divorces, eleven children, and at least eighteen books. In addition to the Mitfords' own memoirs, much has been written about them, both nonfiction and fiction, along with television shows and movies.

If it were not for their politics, the saga of the Mitford girls, as described in the memoirs and in Nancy's novels, would be amusing, in the style of *Life with Father* or *Cheaper by the Dozen*. (Similarly, if it were not for the sex scenes, *Lady Chatterley's Lover* would be an informative study of gamekeeping.) Mary Lovell's is an interesting, well-documented account, written sympathetically and largely without taking sides, although she doesn't seem to care much for the oldest sister, Nancy, while Unity Valkyrie's enthusiasm for Nazis and Nazism obviously upsets her.

The father, David Freeman Mitford, 2nd Lord Redesdale, was an eccentric, crotchety, devoted but tyrannical peer who spent considerable time unsuccessfully working a gold mine in Canada, making poor investments, and campaigning against admission of women peers to the House of Lords on the grounds that they would have to share the sole lavatory. Eventually he bought an island in the Hebrides and lived there. In Nancy's novel *The Pursuit of Love* there is a description of Uncle Matthew, who was modeled on him, and who was "no respecter of other people's early morning sleep, and after five o'clock one could not count on any, for he raged round the house, clanking cups of tea, shouting at his dogs, roaring at the housemaids, cracking the stock whips which he brought back from Canada on the lawn with a noise greater than gun-fire, and all to the accompaniment of Galli-Curci on his gramophone, an abnormally loud one with an enormous horn . . ." (20–21).

The mother, Sydney Bowles, was a woman of narrow views and strong opinions about aristocratic privilege. Apparently she was unable to show affection for her daughters, who believed her cold and censorious, though in later years they decided differently. As war with Germany drew close she continued to insist that Hitler and company meant well, while her husband turned strongly anti-German. The intramural discord was such that they largely ceased trying to live together. After David died, Sydney moved onto the island herself.

The senior Mitfords did not believe in education for women. As Uncle Matthew declares, "You don't have to go to some awful middle-class establishment to know who George III was" (*Pursuit of Love*, 29). There were tutors and governesses, but the girls were not permitted to proceed beyond that, and they deeply resented it. They were also discouraged from making friends among the common sort who resided nearby. Intelligent, imaginative, beautiful, and fully tutored in their social status, they were provided with the intellectual resources and expectations appropriate to the era of George III and left to make their way in the unfolding twentieth century.

Otherwise, as children the sisters were indulged, and if not spoiled, at any rate raised to believe in their own uniqueness, both individually and as a family. In Mary Lovell's words, "there was never any pressure to conform and the children grew as they wanted" (29). There was much teasing and prank-playing. Along with their father's imperiousness and cantankerousness could go considerable indulgence. David Mitford owned a bloodhound, for example, and in one of their favorite games the girls would be the hares; they were given a head start, would run out in the woods and fields, and wait for father and hound to track them down.

The question to ask is not why, when they became adolescents and young adults, they proved to be so extravagantly rebellious (Nancy, Diana, Unity, and Jessica, that is: Pamela and Deborah lived reasonably sedate lives; throughout what follows it will be those first four Mitfords that I shall be writing about). Youthful resentment and insurgency, to be sure, are scarcely remarkable. What is puzzling is the consuming intensity and sustained truculence of the rebellion. It transcended the wish to assert an independence of parental authority, and embodied a craving, even a compulsion, to shock.

What in their father's instance had seemed to be a kind of goofy eccentricity became for them a need to flaunt their obstreperousness, and not merely before their family but upper-class England in general. Glaringly missing from their lives, until well along in years, is any sense of responsibility. To cite the two most obviously flamboyant examples, Unity Valkyrie (Bobo) and Jessica (Decca), there seems to have been a conscious decision to be perceived *as* extremists, to do things that were guaranteed to fly in the face of respectability.

Bobo's passion for Hitler and Nazism was not something that developed over a period of time. Instead, she set out resolutely and consciously to become a Nazi, gain the Führer's acquaintance, and to adopt his racial views and his social program. The violence of her conversion—"I want everyone to know that I am a Jew hater," she wrote to a newspaper in a revealing word choice—is striking, since it is unlikely that she ever had much occasion to be in Jewish company. The intensity of her newfound allegiance embarrassed even her parents, for all that in the 1930s both senior Mitfords were sympathetic to Hitler's political and economic accomplishments in Germany.

Her attitude toward Jews was greatly in excess of the anti-Semitism that characterized so much upper-class British society in the pre–

World War I years and the 1920s, and which was essentially an instinctive response to what was new and seemingly subversive of the established social order. In Unity Mitford's instance there is the distinct sense that cozying up to Nazi racial notions was attractive not from any actual experience of her own, but because it enabled her to do something she could think of as being immoderate and excessive, thus affording her an opportunity to place her recalcitrance on public view. (On one visit home she was doing some target-shooting; questioned by her father, she explained that she was practicing to kill Jews.) The eagerness with which she developed a close friendship with Hitler and other Nazi bigwigs, and the ardor with which she exhibited such friendships, suggests a kind of childlike quest for gratification, as if by misbehaving in public she was fulfilling an intense, infantile personal need.

The coming of war in 1939 spoiled everything. It was one thing to be a self-proclaimed bigot and to seek out the company of doctrinaire Nazis. It was another to become the declared enemy of her country—to commit treason. For much though she publicly endorsed and affirmed the social philosophy of the Master Race, the essence of her rebellion was not ideological but personal. It could be fulfilling for her only to the extent that she could envisage herself as a highborn Briton parading her independence of her family and fellow aristocrats through a defiant approval of Adolf Hitler. Once war was declared that role was no longer feasible, whereupon, in high melodramatic mode, she left instructions that she wished to be buried in Germany with her autographed picture of Hitler and her Nazi Party badge, and with her pearl-handled revolver shot herself in the temple.

She botched the job. Hitler had her hospitalized at his expense and then transferred to Switzerland. "When are you coming to get me?" Mary Lovell reports that she asked plaintively when her parents finally reached her via telephone (304). Brought home to England, thereafter she remained mentally no more than eleven or twelve years old, and was both emotionally erratic and physically incontinent. Cared for by her mother, she died in 1948 after her wound became infected.

In Jessica's (Decca's) instance the motives for her behavior appear equally compulsive. However much her dedication to Marxism and communism may have involved an opposition to fascism and a conviction that British class distinctions were a mask for privilege and injustice, there seems no question that basically what she too was intent upon was conspicuous insurgence. When still twelve years old she set up a "running away" account at the bank. The discovery of an ideology for her rebellion was an outcome, not a cause; there is the sense that because Bobo decided to be a Nazi, Decca opted for communism.

She was fascinated by the antisocial exploits of a cousin, Esmond Romilly, who was Winston Churchill's nephew; Noel Annan calls him "a brigand pillaging the houses of the respectable . . ." (*Our Age* [1990], 184). Upon meeting him Decca asked to be taken to join the Loyalists in the Spanish Civil War. Eventually they ended up in the United States, where they led a hand-to-mouth existence until Esmond enlisted in the Royal Canadian Air Force and in 1941 was lost over the North Sea. When Churchill traveled to Washington after the attack on Pearl Harbor he took time while at the White House to send for Decca and tell her that there was no chance of Esmond's having survived. He also gave her five hundred dollars, part of which she donated to a Communist Party fund.

Afterward she moved to California—it seems an almost inevitable development. She became an American citizen and was remarried, this time to a Harvard-educated Jewish lawyer. She joined the Communist Party, took part in assorted labor and civil rights protests, and during the McCarthy Era ran into trouble, on occasion having to lay low to avoid subpoenas. Her mother, though retaining ultra-conservative views, maintained ties with her, but Decca would not be reconciled with her father, even though unlike her mother he had turned anti-Nazi. Decca's memoir of the family, *Hons and Rebels* (1960; in its American edition *Daughters and Rebels*), and her exposé of the funeral industry, *The American Way of Death* (1963), were both bestsellers. She too celebrated a golden wedding anniversary, but by then, having boozed to excess for too long, was in very poor shape, and died the year following, in 1996. It must be said that whatever its emotional origins, Decca made her rebellion stick.

In the years that followed the end of World War II the one sister with whom she would not renew relations was Diana. Third oldest and the most classically beautiful of the Mitfords, Diana steadfastly defended the life, political career, and social views of her second husband, Sir Oswald Mosley, refusing to concede that he had merited any opprobrium whatever, much less wartime arrest and confinement. Mosley, she insisted, though the leader of Fascist blackshirts, was not anti-Semitic—a claim that her sister Nancy, for one, found preposterous. Diana did concede that numerous of his followers were, which was like admitting that the weather in the British Isles can at times be moist. (Roy Jenkins's description of Mosley is of "a charismatic vulgarian, a visionary who organized thugs . . ." *Baldwin* [1987], 162.)

Diana's first marriage, in 1929, was to Bryan Guinness, heir to an enormous fortune. Three years later she met Mosley. Not only was she dazzled by his swagger and self-assurance, but his social ideas and the glibness with which he expounded them captivated her. Within months she had left her husband, though she and Mosley, who was likewise married at the time, were not formally wedded until 1936. Diana, Unity, and their brother Tom were present for the Nazi Nuremberg rally in 1935, and through Unity, Diana also came to know Hitler quite well. She and Mosley were married in Joseph Goebbels's home, with Hitler in attendance. Diana spent much time in Germany, where she was successful in securing a license for an English-language commercial radio station to furnish revenue for the British Union of Fascists.

When in 1940, following some months of "Phoney War" Hitler's armies barreled through the Low Countries and knocked France out of the war, a German invasion of Britain became a real danger. Mosley was arrested and imprisoned, on the plausible grounds that if invasion did come he might well become a Gauleiter. Diana's frequent visits to Germany and her friendship with leading Nazis also earned imprisonment for her. The Mosleys were not released until 1943, and then in the face of much public and parliamentary protest. In later years Mosley sought unsuccessfully to reenter politics, switched his brand of ethnic extremism from anti-Jew to anti-black, took up the cause of European (as separate from American or Russian) solidarity, and wrote books defending his pre-1939 conduct and advocating his prejudices.

As Mary Lovell suggests, no doubt the key to Diana's writings and public appearances both before and after Mosley's death was the desire to defend his reputation. She even wrote a memoir in which she described the Adolf Hitler of the 1930s as cultured, charming, and fastidious—which supposedly justified the *Kristallnacht* and similar social events.

Nancy Mitford was never able to forgive Mosley for ruining her favorite sister's life. Oldest of the Mitford girls, Nancy felt herself trapped by her dependence upon her family situation, and once she came of age in the early 1920s she was a quick convert to what Martin Green, in *Children of the Sun* (1977), describes as the patent dandyism of the so-called Oxford Wits and kindred souls, "preoccupied with style, [who] worshipped Adonis or Narcissus, were rebellious against both their fathers' and their mothers' modes of seriousness, were in love with ornament, splendour, high manners, and so on . . ." (26). Their frequent presence at the family home often enraged David Freeman Mitford. In 1933, after a futile love affair with a homosexual, Nancy was married on the rebound to Peter Rodd, described by Mary Lovell as "an arrogant and pedantic know-it-all" (152). By the late 1930s this had ended, though not until the 1950s was their divorce made final.

She published her first novel in 1935, but it was with *The Pursuit of Love* (1947) that she became a best-selling novelist, drawing extensively and cleverly upon her parents, family, and upper-tier British life for her material. This was followed by several other novels, all of them, to quote the jacket of *The Nancy Mitford Omnibus* (1986), "scintillating novels of love and high society." There were also biographies of Frederick the Great, Madame Pompadour, and Voltaire, all successful. Perhaps her widest fame came from the article in *Noblesse Oblige* (1956). Identifying what was "U" and what was "non-U" became a parlor pastime both in Great Britain and the United States.

While working in London during the war, Nancy met the love of her life, Gaston Palewski, Charles de Gaulle's cabinet chief. The Colonel, as she called him, was fond of her, but made it clear that marriage was not in the cards. She moved to Paris in 1946, and thereafter until her death in 1973 maintained her ties with the Colonel, even after, to her considerable anguish, he was married. For most of those years she cut a wide path in Anglo-French artistic circles.

Politics were not of primary importance in Nancy's life. She tended toward socialism in the abstract, was anti-Nazi and anti-Communist, and detested Oswald Mosley and the British Union of

Fascists. When war broke out she did not hesitate to inform the government about her sister Diana's numerous visits to Germany and to warn that she was a "very dangerous person." In this she was joined by family friends and by Diana's ex-father-in-law.

For all of the fun she made of her parents and of the English aristocracy, Nancy herself appears to have been a Grade-A1 snob, and her fiction is steeped in the extravagances of rank and class, based obviously on a sense of amused self-recognition. Her archness was part of her personality from youth onward; it appears to have been a way of masking her own emotional vulnerability. Her mother complained that her letters always contained a barb. With her close friend and correspondent Evelyn Waugh she traded wickedly clever commentary. Decidedly middle-class in background himself but socially very ambitious, Waugh both admired her lofty status and took satisfaction in knowing that of the two, he was the greater literary artist—as Nancy would readily have agreed. But where Waugh was a compulsive misanthrope who was capable of genuine malevolence, Nancy was probably more reflexively sardonic than cruel.

In a very real way, what for Nancy was converted into literary comedy was in its emotional origins based at least in part on the same impulse that in Diana, Unity Valkyrie, and Decca took the form of a craving to shock respectable opinion. All four of them were bent upon Causing A Stir, whether artistically as with Nancy, or politically and socially as with the others. In each instance the confidence of possessing indisputable social rank, however they might deride and flout it, underlay their actions and assumptions. There is the sense, at every stage in their careers, of *divertissement,* of role-playing.

This is not to say that they were insincere, or that they did not work hard at and even suffer for their chosen enterprises. But in next to nothing of what any of them did or thought—except possibly for Nancy—can the presence of humility be discovered. The rebellious Mitford girls—again, not including Pamela or Debo—may not always have known what they wanted, but whatever it was, it never occurred to them that they did not possess an inherited right to it. If what they sought was not immediately forthcoming—in the form, that is, that they had been taught to expect it—then they would go after it, without so much as a moment's concern for anyone else's feelings. Nancy alone of them seems ever to have begun to perceive the limitations of that approach.

Mary Lovell has done her best by them. Still, when all is said and done, the sum total of their joint performance, again with the intermittent exception of Nancy, was self-indulgence.

As antidote to the four Mitfords, I recommend the three volumes of Mark Pottle's selections from the diaries and letters of Violet Asquith Bonham Carter: *Lantern Slides: The Diaries and Letters of Violet Bonham Carter, 1904–1914,* edited by Mark Bonham Carter and Mark Pottle (1996); *Champion Redoubtable: The Diaries and Letters of Violet Bonham Carter, 1914–1945,* edited by Mark Pottle (1998); *Daring to Hope: The Diaries and Letters of Violet Bonham Carter, 1946–1969,* edited by Mark Pottle (2000). Together they constitute a running chronicle of upper-class British public and private life for the better portion of the twentieth century.

Violet Bonham Carter was not of aristocratic descent on either side of her family, but when she was a small girl her mother died and her father married into the higher reaches of the Establishment. In upbringing, attitudes, and assumptions Violet was, to use Nancy Mitford's formulation, "U" rather than "non-U." For her part, she was able to do what the Mitford girls largely could not: find a vocation that was both emotionally and intellectually fulfilling.

If so, the case can be made that her highly useful life and career were in no small way made possible because of her social situation. Instead of being used by it, however, she used it. She seems to me to represent the English Establishment at its most attractive. As for the Mitfords, or at least for several of them, one is tempted to say, along with David Cannadine, let the decline and fall continue.

The much-admired daughter of a prime minister, Violet came to be nearly everything that the Mitford girls largely were not, which is to say, a woman of social and political responsibility, high personal integrity, and goodwill. She learned to use her privileged status not for caprice and self-pleasuring but in order to lead a life of useful involvement. In certain respects she reminds one of Eleanor Roosevelt; if so, she possessed something of the same ability to upset and infuriate the Old Guard.

It was her son Mark Bonham Carter's idea to publish his mother's diaries and letters, but he died before the first volume appeared. Mark Pottle, the editor, has throughout provided passages of historical continuity, informative but not obtrusive annotation, biographical sketches of the more important persons figuring in Violet Bonham Carter's life, and glossaries of people, places, and terms. The editing is a model of its kind; I have not encountered better.

Violet Asquith was born in 1887. Herbert Henry Asquith, her father, was solidly middle class in background, as was her mother, who died when she was four years old. Three years later her father, a rising Liberal politician with no inconsiderable element of social ambition in his makeup, married Margot Tennant, daughter of a wealthy Scots industrialist and a much-talked-about figure in fashionable late Victorian English society. Violet's upbringing was definitely upper-middle and solidly within the Establishment, and the diary entries and letters of her younger years frequently display some of its allegiances and its prejudices. There is the characteristic assumption that the world was there for her convenience, the patronizing attitude toward the Lower Orders, the reflexive anti-Semitism, and so on.

One would scarcely guess that the gushing rhapsode who wrote the starry-eyed diary entries of Volume I, *Lantern Slides,* would become the clear-sighted, outspoken champion of rearmament and foe of appeasement who joined her lifelong friend Winston Churchill in standing up to Nazi Germany in the 1930s, and who in the 1940s and 1950s headed the Liberal Party Organization in Great Britain. Indeed, it is scarcely too much to say that her career did much that would securely establish the role of women in English public life—and this even though prior to 1914, in the time of the suffragettes, she opposed extension of the franchise to women.

She was in her late teens in 1905 when H. H. Asquith was made chancellor of the exchequer. In 1908 he succeeded Henry Campbell-Bannerman as prime minister. During the decade of 1905–1914 the Liberals achieved an outstanding social and political record. The power of the nonelected House of Lords to block the reforms of the elected House of Commons was decisively and permanently curbed. Old-age pensions, free school meals, labor exchanges, national health insurance for certain workers, and a greater proportionate share of taxation for the very wealthy were enacted, along with a notably expanded battle fleet to counter the ominous increase in German naval strength. Asquith guided his party through all these developments, with David Lloyd George and the young Winston Churchill playing key roles in the Liberal cabinet.

Asquith's parliamentary and political skills proved to be less well adapted to the demands of leadership once war broke out in 1914. For an embattled nation his conciliatory, easygoing style failed to communicate the urgency of the struggle and to dramatize the need for precedent-shattering effort. In 1915, after the failure of the Dardanelles campaign, he was forced into accepting a coalition government, for which Churchill had long been pressing. Ironically, the price of Conservative Party participation was the ouster of Churchill from the Admiralty. Late the following year Asquith himself was maneuvered out of No. 10 Downing Street in favor of Lloyd George, a man of fewer professional or ethical scruples, greater administrative talents, and a driving determination to do whatever was necessary to win the war, without concern for individual reputations or private sensibilities. Never again would H. H. Asquith be part of a government, or the Liberal Party ever be empowered to form one.

Violet Asquith adored her father, who in her eyes could do no wrong; throughout her long life she was quick to protest any disparagement of his record and reputation. (Her opposition to women's suffrage in the 1910s was doubtless the result of her father's opposition to it, and perhaps the severe harassment he received from militant suffragettes. On one occasion she came to his defense when he was physically assaulted while on a golf course.)

Early on she demonstrated a talent for public speaking, and before very long was appearing regularly at election rallies on behalf of not only her father but also other Liberal candidates for parliamentary seats. As her friend Churchill wrote, in the 1920s "[h]er father—old, supplanted in power, his party broken up, his authority flouted, even his long-faithful constituency estranged—found in his daughter a champion redoubtable even in the first rank of party orators" (*Great Contemporaries* [1937], 115).

It has been speculated that in her youthful years she was in love with Churchill, whom she greatly admired, and that probably she would have married him if asked, but general agreement has it that physical attraction was not a compelling element in their close friendship. When Churchill married Clementine Hozier, a touch of backbiting does surface in Violet's response. In any event, the thought of two strong-willed, outspoken activists such as Winston Churchill and Violet Asquith as man and wife is awesome to contemplate.

She did not lack for suitors, and during the prewar years seems to have come close to marriage herself on several occasions. The strongest rival that any of her suitors faced, however, was her own father, the prime minister, who relied upon her companionship, and who on at least one occasion when she contemplated marrying, begged her not to desert him. Asquith was to an inordinate degree dependent upon female company; habitually he maintained a lengthy correspondence with various women, and his acquaintances spoke of his "harem."

By 1914 he had become deeply involved emotionally with a friend of Violet's, Venetia Stanley, with whom he corresponded on almost a daily basis, often writing to her during cabinet meetings. When in 1915 Venetia announced her intention to marry Edwin Montagu, Asquith's loyal Liberal Party associate, the impact of the news upon Asquith's morale was devastating. The disclosure came just when the Dardanelles debacle was looming, Conservative attacks on Churchill were growing serious, and the Liberal government appeared (and was) about to yield its sole control of government to a multiparty coalition.

In order to marry Montagu, whose father's will provided that any of his children who married out of the family faith were not to receive income from his considerable estate, Venetia had agreed to convert to Judaism. Violet fastened upon the religious conversion as dishonest, hypocritical, the betrayal of principle for financial gain, and so on. In any event, Venetia's move appears to have jarred Violet loose from her own emotional impasse, and within days she had accepted Maurice Bonham Carter's suit. When they were married in November of 1915, her father wrote to "beg and pray of you to keep our divine companionship as it has always been. Something has to be sacrificed: but let the essential & true thing be always there" (*Champion Redoubtable*, 115).

After World War I, following the rise of a separate Labour Party that was to an important degree controlled by the increasingly powerful trade unions, the Liberals split into Asquith and Lloyd George factions. Caught between the dominant allegiances of left and right, they were never to regain their status as a major party.

Asquith died in 1928. Throughout the 1920s, and thereafter for the next four decades, Violet played a leading role in the Liberal Party. She was urged by Margot Asquith, her stepmother, and by various

Liberal politicians to become a candidate for Parliament herself, but she insisted that her first duty was to her children, of whom by 1929 there were four. Nowadays no such home-vs.-career choice would have been necessary—or, more accurately perhaps, would have seemed to her to be necessary.

From the late 1920s through the decade of the 1930s she apparently did not keep a diary, nor do many letters from that period survive.* There was a cooling of her friendship with Churchill following his switch to the Conservatives and his acceptance of the chancellorship of the exchequer under Stanley Baldwin in 1924, but the rise of Nazism in Germany in the early 1930s brought them together again. Even before Churchill did, she recognized the menace of Hitler's Third Reich and began speaking out against it. In May of 1933 she warned the Liberal Party that "In Germany freedom as we conceive it seems to have perished in the last few weeks, in the twinkling of an eye, almost without a struggle, & given place to a nightmare reign of force whose horror we can hardly conceive . . . " (*Champion Redoubtable,* 181). Shocked by the Nazi persecution of Jews, she took a leading part in establishing a fund to aid refugees. She gave vigorous support to Churchill's anti-appeasement stand, denounced Neville Chamberlain's Munich agreement with Hitler as a betrayal of freedom, and called for a coalition to oppose any further Conservative accommodation with totalitarianism.

In May of 1940, when France crumpled before the German assault and Churchill became prime minister, she rejoiced: "He will indeed have to ride the whirlwind & direct the storm," she wrote in her diary. "If any man can he will, but he has as a heritage the years that the locust has eaten" (*Champion Redoubtable,* 212). The year following, a Liberal parliamentary seat fell vacant and she hoped to receive the nomination, which was tantamount to election, but it went to someone else. During the war she served as a governor of the British Broadcasting Corporation and, with her husband, as air-raid warden. Her son Mark was captured in North Africa and imprisoned in Italy, from where he escaped and made it back to England. A son-in-law, Jasper Ridley, was less lucky; also captured and held in Italy, he was killed while attempting to escape through a minefield.

*It is possible that a long-standing affair with Hugh Godley may explain why so few letters from these years are included in the Violet Bonham Carter papers at the Bodleian Library

When the fighting was over in Europe she wrote to Churchill that "you have led, inspired, sustained us *as no other could have done.* This war began long before 1939. You were leading us then—& I am proud to have been with you from the start to this our Journey's End" (*Champion Redoubtable,* 345). Violet had deplored Churchill's decision to assume the leadership of the Conservative Party after Neville Chamberlain's death, as had Clementine Churchill, and now she regretted her friend's decision to fight the 1945 general election as a Tory partisan. He was not "one of them," she insisted, meaning the right-wing Conservatives who had sought to appease Hitler in the 1930s. As it was, the Liberals were forced to contest the election independently rather than as part of a coalition, and not only Violet and her son Mark but numerous other Liberals seeking seats in Parliament lost out in the Labour Party's victory.

It was in the decades following the end of World War II that Violet enjoyed her greatest prominence and effectiveness in British political life. She became the first woman president of the Liberal Party Organization and regularly took to the hustings in support of various Liberal candidates, including son Mark and her son-in-law Jo Grimond, who was twice elected parliamentary leader of the Liberals. It was necessary for Mark to forbid her, at age seventy-seven and in failing health, from taking part in his own campaign. She was active in championing the cause of the Republic of Israel, opposed the British-French intervention in Suez, fought apartheid in South Africa and anti-immigration laws in England, and campaigned against capital punishment.

She lectured in Europe and America; on a trip to Washington she met and was tremendously impressed with President Kennedy. Her husband, Sir Maurice Bonham-Carter, died in 1960. In 1964 she was made a lifetime peer, taking the title of Lady Asquith of Yarnbury, thereafter participating actively in the Lords' deliberations. After Churchill's death she published a book, *Winston Churchill As I Knew Him* (1965). She spoke often on radio, was a frequent panelist on television, and in January of 1969, less than three weeks before she died at age eighty-one, made it to a theater to take part in a BBC documentary, *An Evening with Lady Asquith,* which was broadcast after her death.

As all who knew her readily conceded, she was one of a kind. She held strong views, and throughout her life was in no way backward in voicing them. She would hear nothing favorable about Lloyd George or the Tory Party. On one occasion, when a young journalist, Quentin Crewe, who had lived with the Bonham Carters, announced that he was writing for a newspaper that supported the Conservatives editorially, she tore into him: "That you, who come from a good Liberal family, that you, who have lived in my house, that you, whom I have trusted and been fond of, should sink to working for that organ of evil, is more than I can bear." But later, after Crewe had written a piece poking fun at a Conservative Party conference, she wrote to tell him that it was "brilliantly amusing . . ." (Crewe, *Well, I Forget the Rest* [1991], 56–57).

That she was a formidable and even something of a knee-jerk advocate of Worthy Causes is undeniable. To those in positions of authority who were required to cope with a less-than-perfect world, this could be exasperating. To cite only one instance, during the invasion of North Africa in 1942, in order to end French resistance to the landings and save numerous lives the Anglo-American headquarters arranged a deal with Jean Darlan, the Vichy French admiral. Violet joined in the chorus of those who protested the seeming "betrayal" of war aims, and at a wedding party apparently confronted Clementine Churchill about it. "I had a short interchange with Clemmie over Darlan," she recorded in her diary, "in which she—to my amazement—completely lost her temper & nearly emptied a glass of champagne over herself & me saying 'I used to think you were an intelligent woman!'" (*Champion Redoubtable,* 248). The episode, and her surprise, may help to explain why her son-in-law, Jo Grimond, described her as "curiously innocent" (384).

She was a highly effective platform advocate, and although at times her outspokenness on occasions both public and private could no doubt be trying, she was generous, loyal, good-hearted, and cared deeply for others. What she possessed to a notable degree was the capacity for growth; she was open to new experience, and willing, even eager, to learn from it. The range of her sympathies expanded with the years. Inheriting the attitudes of upper-tier England in what during her early years was a society steeped in class, caste, and privilege, she came to recognize and to discount the limitations of much of that inheritance, while continuing to be what and who she so vigorously was. To read the successive volumes of her diary and letters is to follow the development of a vibrant woman, attractive, emotionally passionate and intellectually intense, as she experienced and took part in the unfolding decades of the twentieth century from a vantage point that brought her into continued touch with the important and influential in British public life.

She was, and she remained, a product of her time, place, and favored social position. Paradoxically her privileged status might be said to have been what enabled her to open the way for a woman whose views and social attitudes she would have abhorred, Margaret Thatcher. Surely the prime minister under whose leadership the Conservative Party won three general elections, and who lacked any such social auspices as Violet enjoyed, would have found it far harder to make her way in British party politics had it not been for Violet's pioneering precedence. Yet had Violet not enjoyed, by inheritance and upbringing, the ready access to circles of power and influence that came with her ties to the Liberal Party elite, it seems doubtful that her own career would have developed as it did. Still, other women had similar ties. It was Violet Bonham Carter who made them work for her.

Characteristic of her sensibility is a remark in her diary for Friday, January 29, 1965, describing the scene where the body of Churchill lay in state:

> The unbroken human stream flowed on. It was so strange to think that *W.* was lying there—high up in that vast coffin—under its Union Jack—He wld. have been moved by the people & the love he had inspired. I said to Mark afterwards that nothing has ever given me a more *uncomfortable* sense of undue "privilege" than being able to slip in & out (& take anyone I like with me—up to 6 people) while these others had queued for miles & hours in icy rain & bitter wind. (*Daring to Hope*, 300)

It would be difficult to imagine a similar reflection on the part of any of the Mitfords.

Works Cited

A Certain Day in 1939

Von Kolnitz, Major Alfred H. *The Battery in Charleston, South Carolina: Three Centuries of History.* Charleston, 1937.

The Summer the Archduke Died

Cecil, Lamar. *Wilhelm II: Prince and Emperor, 1859–1900.* Chapel Hill, N.C., 1989.

Cecil, Lamar. *Wilhelm II: Emperor and Exile, 1941–1946.* Chapel Hill, N.C., 1996.

Geiss, Immanuel. "The Outbreak of the First World War and German War Aims," in Walter Laqueur and George L. Mosse, eds., *1914: The Coming of the First World War.* New York, 1966.

Hillgruber, Andreas. *Germany and the Two World Wars.* Cambridge, Mass., 1981.

Jarausch, Konrad H. *The Enigmatic Chancellor: Bethmann Hollweg and the Hubris of Imperial Germany.* New Haven, Conn., 1972.

Röhl, John C. G. "Germany," in Keith Wilson, ed., *Decisions for War, 1914.* New York, 1995.

Strachan, Hew. *The First World War.* Vol. I: *To Arms.* New York, 2001.

Taylor, A. J. "War by Time-Table," in Chris Wrigley, ed., *From the Boer War to the Cold War: Essays on Twentieth-Century Europe.* New York, 1995.

Trachtenberg, Marc. "The Meaning of Mobilization in 1914," in Steven E. Miller, Sean M. Lynn-Jones, and Stephen Van Evera, eds., *Military Strategy and the Origins of the First World War.* Revised and expanded edition. Princeton, N.J., 1991.

Tuchman, Barbara W. *The Guns of August.* New York, 1962.

Van der Kisle, John. *Kaiser Wilhelm II, Germany's Last Emperor.* Gloucestershire, Eng., 1999.

Williamson, Samuel R., Jr. *Austria-Hungary and the Origins of the First World War.* New York, 1991.

Williamson, Samuel R., Jr. *The Politics of Grand Strategy: Britain and France Prepare for War, 1904–1914.* London, 1990.

"The Weasel's Twist, the Weasel's Tooth"

Falls, Cyril. *The Great War, 1914–1918.* New York, 1959.

Gibbons, Floyd. *The Red Knight of Germany: The Story of Baron von Richthofen.* New York, 1927.

Gilbert, Martin. *The First World War: A Complete History.* New York, 1995.

Letters of Henry James. Edited by Percy Lubbock. 2 vols. New York, 1920.

High Tide at Jutland

Campbell, N. J. M. *Jutland: An Analysis of the Fighting.* Annapolis, Md., 1986.

Churchill, Winston S. *The World Crisis and the Aftermath, 1911–1918.* 4 vols. New York, 1923–1927.

Gordon, Andrew. *The Rules of the Game: Jutland and British Naval Command.* Annapolis, Md., 1996.

The Holstein Papers: Correspondence. Edited by Norman Rich and M. H. Fisher. 4 vols. Cambridge, Eng., 1963.

Hough, Richard. *The Great War at Sea, 1914–1918.* New York, 1983.

Marder, Arthur J. *From the Dreadnought to Scapa Flow: The Royal Navy in the Fisher Era, 1904–1919.* 5 vols. London, 1961–1970.

Massie, Robert. *Dreadnought: Britain, Germany, and the Coming of the Great War.* New York, 1991.

Tarrant, V. E. *Jutland: The German Perspective: A New View of the Great Battle, 31 May 1916.* Annapolis, Md.: 1995.

Western Front: The Americans Enter the War

Braim, Paul F. *The Test of Battle: The American Expeditionary Forces in the Meuse-Argonne Campaign.* Newark, Del., 1987.
Farwell, Byron. *Over There: The United States in the Great War, 1917–1918.* New York, 1999.
Harries, Meirion, and Susie Harries. *The Last Days of Innocence: America at War, 1917–1918.* New York, 1997.
Johnson, Hubert C. *Breakthrough!: Tactics, Technology, and the Search for Victory on the Western Front in World War I.* Novato, Calif., 1994.
Keegan, John. *The First World War.* New York, 1999.
May, Henry F. *The End of American Innocence: A Study of the First Years of Our Own Time.* New York, 1959.

Literature and the Great War

Fussell, Paul. *The Great War and Modern Memory.* New York, 1975.
Hynes, Samuel. *A War Imagined: The First World War and English Culture.* 1991.
Paschall, Rod. *The Defeat of Imperial Germany, 1917–1918.* Chapel Hill, N.C., 1989.
Brooks, Cleanth, and Robert Penn Warren. *Understanding Poetry: An Anthology for College Students.* Revised edition. New York, 1950.

T. R.

Blum, John M. *Joe Tumulty and the Wilson Era.* Boston, 1951.
Butt, Archibald W. *The Letters of Archie Butt: Personal Aide to President Roosevelt.* Edited by Lawrence F. Abbott. New York, 1924.
Cooper, John Milton. *The Warrior and the Priest.* Cambridge, Mass.: 1983.

Dalton, Kathleen. *Theodore Roosevelt: A Strenuous Life.* New York, 2002.

McCullough, David. *Mornings On Horseback.* New York, 2001.

Morris, Edmund. *Theodore Rex.* New York, 2001.

Mowry, George. *The Era of Theodore Roosevelt and the Birth of Modern America, 1912–1958.* New York, 1958.

Pershing, John J. *My Experiences in the World War.* 2 vols. New York, 1931.

Selected Writing of Theodore Roosevelt: A Reader. Edited by Bryan M. Thomsen. New York, 2003.

Wister, Owen. *Roosevelt: The Story of a Friendship.* New York, 1930.

Zimmerman, Warren. *First Great Triumph: How Five Americans Made Their Country a World Power.* New York, 2002.

Did Churchill "Ruin the Great Work of Time"?

Cannadine, David. *The Decline and Fall of the British Aristocracy.* New York, 1990.

Charmley, John. *Churchill: The End of Glory.* New York, 1993.

Cooper, Matthew. *The German Army: Its Political and Military Failure, 1933–1945.* New York, 1978.

Ladies of the English Establishment

Annan, Noel. *Our Age: British Intellectuals between the Two Wars—A Group Portrait.* London, 1994.

Bonham Carter, Violet. *Lantern Slides: The Diaries and Letters of Violet Bonham Carter, 1904–1914.* Edited by Mark Bonham Carter and Mark Pottle. London, 1996.

Bonham Carter, Violet. *Champion Redoubtable: The Diaries and Letters of Violet Bonham Carter, 1914–1945.* Edited by Mark Pottle. London, 1998.

Bonham Carter, Violet. *Daring to Hope: The Diaries and Letters of Violet Bonham Carter, 1946–1969.* Edited by Mark Pottle. London, 2000.

Cannadine, David. *Aspects of Aristocracy: Grandeur and Decline in Modern Britain.* New Haven, Conn., 1994.

Cannadine, David. *The Decline and Fall of the British Aristocracy.* New Haven, Conn., 1990.

Cannadine, David. *The Rise and Fall of Class in Britain.* New Haven, Conn., 1999.

Churchill, Winston. *Great Contemporaries.* New York, 1937.

Green, Martin. *Children of the Sun: A Narrative of "Decadence" in England after 1918.* London, 1977.

Crewe, Quentin, *Well, I Forget the Rest: The Autobiography of an Optimist.* London, 1991.

Jenkins, Roy. *Baldwin.* London, 1987.

Lovell, Mary S. *The Sisters: The Saga of the Mitford Family.* New York, 2002.

Mitford, Nancy. *Pursuit of Love: A Novel.* London, 1945.

Index

Index 163

Jutland: An Analysis of the Fighting (Campbell), 56–57

Jutland: An Analysis of the Fighting (Campbell), 56–57
Jutland: The German Perspective (Tarrant), 56

Kaiser Wilhelm II (Van der Kiste), 24
Kaisershymne (Haydn), 68
Kansas City, Mo., 82
Keegan, John, 64–73, 82
Kemal, Mustapha, 71
Kind Hearts and Coronets (Guinness), 60
Knox, Frank, 113
Kolnitz, Alfred H. von, 3
König, SMS, 57
Korean War, 130
Krystallnacht, 143

Labour Party, 122, 133, 148
Lady Chatterley's Lover (Lawrence), 137–38
La Follette, Robert, 109
Lantern Slides (Bonham Carter and Pottle), 145ff
Laqueur, George, 27
Last Days of American Innocence, The (Harries), 72ff
Lawrence, D. H., 90–91, 137–38
League of Nations, 108–109
Leningrad, battle of, 126
Letters of Archie Butt (Abbott), 105, 114–15
Letters of Henry James (Lubbock), 35
Lewis, Wyndham, 90
Leyte Gulf, battle of, 33
Liberal Party, 133, 146ff
Liege, battle of, 65
Liggett, Hunter, 80
Lion, HMS, 50–51
Lion's Pride, The (Renehan), 98
Lloyd George, David, 146–51
Longworth, Alice Roosevelt, 104
Loos, battle of, 40
Lords, House of, 133–36, 138, 146, 150
Lorraine, 69–70
Louis XIV, King, 45
Love in a Cold Climate (Mitford), 136
Lubbock, Percy, 35

Ludendorff, Erich, 70ff, 86
Lusitania, 55, 108
Lützow, SMS, 51
Luxembourg, invasion of, 25, 70

MacArthur, Charles, 81
Magic Mountain (Mann), 31
Mahan, Alfred T., 62
Man in the Arena, The (Thomsen), 98
Mann, Thomas, 31
Manual of Fleet Evolutions (Colomb), 59
Marder, Arthur, 56ff, 61
Markham, Albert, 59–60
Marlborough, HMS, 52
Marne, battles of, 71ff, 80, 94
Marshall Plan, 119
Marvell, Andrew, 116
Marxism, 18,46, 18, 147. *See also* Soviet Union
Massie, Robert, 46
May, Henry W., 79, 92–93
McCarthy, Joseph, 141
McCullough, David, 98, 104
McDanel, Ralph C., 31
McKinley, William, 99, 114
Mediterranean Sea, 27, 127
Melville, Herman, 1, 93
Mencken, H. L., 106, 118
Metz, 75
Meuse-Argonne, 7, 72ff, 84–85
Midway, battle of, 33
Military Strategy and the Origins of the First World War (Miller), 28
Miller, Stephen E., 28
Minsk, battle of, 126
Mitford, David Freeman, 138–39
Mitford, Deborah, 137ff
Mitford, Diana Mosley, 137ff
Mitford, Jessica, 137ff
Mitford, Nancy, 134–45
Mitford, Pamela, 137ff
Mitford, Sydney Bowles, 136ff
Mitford, Thomas, 136, 142
Mitford, Unity Valkyrie, 137ff
Mitford family, 136ff
Mobile Bay, battle of, 7
Modern literature, and World War I, 35, 40, 49, 83–96, 131–32
Modernism, in art, 88ff, 93ff, 131–32